Praise for Frank Brennan's *Amplifying That Still Small Voice:*

Members of the Australian public, our fellow citizens of Australia, crave leadership and examples of how to openly, honestly, and fully form a conscience and arrive at a conscientious decision. When I was in parliament, Frank Brennan, to me, always stood as an example of how to do this, and more importantly, the insistence that this must always be done. In fact, I regarded him as a bit of a hero.
    -Kristina Keneally, ex-Premier of NSW

I have taken great pride in being able to claim brotherhood with the author as a Jesuit. Frank Brennan has walked the Australian stage invited to address a whole range of believers and unbelievers, invited because of their respect for his erudition and integrity, and the values and background out of which he speaks.
    -Bishop Greg O'Kelly SJ AM

Frank is not afraid to hold his church, his society and indeed the community of nations up to the gold standard of the dignity and freedom of the individual.
    -Mr Paul Bongiorno AM, Journalist

By personal example and from the richness of his own reflective spirituality, Frank Brennan refuses to allow the perspective of Christianity to be drowned out or sidelined in Australian public discourse. As much as any other religious figure in Australia, Frank has maintained this religious perspective while engaging in issues of ethics and justice in contemporary Australia.
    -Brother Sean McManus cfc

Maintaining a Convinced and Pondered Trust

The 2015 Gasson Lectures

Maintaining a Convinced and Pondered Trust

The 2015 Gasson Lectures

Frank Brennan SJ

ATF Theology
Adelaide
2015

Text copyright © 2015 remains with Frank Brennan SJ.

All rights reserved. Except for any fair dealing permitted under the Copyright Act, no part of this book may be reproduced by any means without prior permission. Inquiries should be made to the publisher.

National Library of Australia Cataloguing-in-Publication
Creator: Brennan, Frank, 1954- author.

Title: Maintaining a convinced and pondered trust : the 2015 Gasson lectures / Frank Brennan.

ISBN: 9781925232615 (paperback)
9781925232622 (hardback)
9781925232639 (ebook : kindle)
9781925232646 (ebook : pdf)

Notes: Includes index.

Subjects: Common good--Religious aspects--Catholic Church.
Euthanasia.
Assisted suicide.
Political refugees.
Refugees.

Other Creators/Contributors:
Gasson lectures.

Dewey Number: 261.7
Creator: Brennan, Frank, 1954- author.

Cover design and Layout/Artwork by Astrid Sengkey

Author photo credit Kylie Ball, and front cover credit is Professor Michael Noone.
Text Minion Pro Size 10 &11

Published by:

An imprint of the ATF Ltd.
PO Box 504
Hindmarsh, SA 5007
ABN 90 116 359 963
www.atfpress.com
Making a lasting impact

*Dedicated to
Jim Keenan SJ, David Hollenbach SJ, John Paris SJ,
and Kenneth Himes ofm
who each decade have provided intellectual refreshment and
fraternal hospitality at Roberts House*

Table of Contents

Foreword by Professor James Keenan SJ	ix
Introduction: Having Space and Thriving on Difference	xiii
Chapter 1: Human Dignity and Public Order	1
Chapter 2: Autonomy and the Common Good *The case study of law and policy relating to euthanasia and physician assisted suicide*	27
—Response by Professor Margaret Somerville	57
Chapter 3: Human rights and the National Interest *The Case study of asylum, migration and national border protection*	69
—Response by Professor Mary Ellen O'Connell	111
Conclusion: Having an Assured Place Informing Public Policy and Law Making	117
Contributors	125
Index	127

Foreword

In 1979 Boston College appointed its first Gasson Professor, the economist, Fr William Neenan, SJ. The Professorship, named after Fr Thomas Gasson, SJ (1859–1930), is the oldest endowed professorship at Boston College.

Fr Gasson is celebrated at Boston College because he moved the university from its downtown campus in Boston to Chestnut Hill. He was born in Kent, England, and arrived in the United States at the age of thirteen. He taught at several Jesuit institutions both in America and in Austria before being made professor of ethics and economics at Boston College in 1895.

Discussions about the need for a larger campus had been going on for at least a decade before Fr Gasson became Boston College's 13th president in 1907. Within a few months, the new leader was proposing the purchase of several parcels of land on Commonwealth Avenue and Beacon Street in Chestnut Hill. His vision was extensive; he argued that not only should a new campus be secured, but also that numerous buildings be constructed, distinguished lay professors be hired, and an expanded program in the natural sciences be established.

Today many attribute to Fr Gasson a vision of Boston College as a global institution. That global vision underlies the Gasson Professorship that is a one or two-year appointment to recruit a world-class Jesuit academic to serve at Boston College in his own particular academic competence, with special attention to delivering the annual Gasson lecture.

To know the Gasson Professorship is to know those who have held the position. A good introduction is found through Fr Neenan who tells the story of how he was recruited:

> I was at Michigan 15 years, and I loved being there, and I got tenure, and one day I got a call from an economist at Boston College whom I'd met while I was on a fellowship in Washington, and he said, Bill, the Jesuits have endowed a professorship called the Gasson Professor for a Jesuit in any discipline, and we'd like to nominate you. I said, fine. And I had literally forgotten about this and was trying to finish a book, and he called and told me I had been selected as Gasson professor. Gasson? I didn't know what Gasson was. So that's how I came.[1]

Subsequent to holding the chair, Neenan remained at the university, held a series of administrative appointments, and became arguably the most beloved of all administrators until his death in 2014. With Neenan, there developed a secondary purpose for awarding the Gasson Professorship: the recruitment of Jesuit faculty to Boston College. Thus six years after Neenan, Fr J Robert Barth, SJ, highly regarded for his expertise in the works of literary figures such as Samuel Coleridge and Gerard Manley Hopkins, was awarded the chair and was subsequently appointed to the university. Among other offices, Fr Barth was the Dean of the School of Arts and Sciences from 1989-1999. In 1997, Fr Richard Blake, a noted film critic was appointed to the professorship and he too later joined the Boston College faculty.

In 2001, Boston College appointed its first alumnus to the position, Fr Paul McNelis, a scholar of econometrics, international macroeconomics and finance, who had taught at Georgetown since 1977. McNelis held degrees in philosophy and economics from Boston College and his doctorate from Johns Hopkins University.

Some major American theologians have been among Boston College's Gasson Professors. In 1981 Fr Avery Dulles was appointed and from 1987–1989 the Scripture scholar Joseph Fitzmeyer held the position. The renowned church historian John O'Malley was also a Gasson Professor in 1992–1993.

More recently there have been Jesuit faculty recruited from outside the United States. In 2005 the theologian Jose Mario Francisco, from the Philippines was recruited and in 2007, Father Rene Javellana, SJ, a

---

1. http://bcm.bc.edu/issues/summer_2014/features/william-b-neenan-sj-1929-2014.html#sthash.TvyWQ6Db.dpuf.

professor of fine arts, presented the Gasson lecture on the Philippine Cinema.

In 2009, Fr Andrea Vicini, an Italian Jesuit, a trained physician specialising in pediatrics and a theological ethicist received the appointment and afterwards joined the Faculty of the School of Theology and Ministry. Vicini did his doctoral studies at Boston College. In 2012 Philip Endean, the English professor of Ignatian spirituality was the Gasson Professor.

Before Endean, the 2011–12 Gasson Professorship had two notable firsts with the appointment of the composer Christopher Willcock: Willcock was the first Australian Jesuit to be appointed and the first Gasson professor to be housed in the music.

Future appointments include this year, 2015–2016, the political scientist Pierre De Charentenay who was the editor of *Etudes* from 2004-2012 and now is among the college of writers for the monthly *Civilta Cattolica* in Rome. In 2016, the Gasson lectures will be given by the scholar of Islam, Gerhard Bowering from Yale University. In 2017, from India Francis Xavier, founder-director of Loyola-ICAM College of Engineering and Technology in Chennai, will assume the position.

But you are interested in this year's Gasson Professor, Frank Brennan. With *Maintaining a Convinced and Pondered Trust,* Frank Brennan remarkably changed the Gasson Lecture from a single event into a series. Only Frank's extraordinary intelligence, extroversion, and complete dedication to engaged and transparent legal investigation could proffer a triple exercise, as he has done here.

I know Frank as a brother Jesuit, a community member, and as an academic colleague. In each context, I know Frank as he is. Transparency is a quality that is natural for him; it would be hard for Frank to be false. What you see is what you get.

Because of that transparency, he was able, I think, in all three lectures to provide that 'fresh perspective' that is a Brennan trademark, an ability to revisit the well-known in a way that nothing seems tired and because everything is well, urgent. He did that on all three topics, the general one on human dignity, the case study highlighting the tension between autonomy and the common good, and the incredibly moving engagement with the plight of refugees and immigrants struggling for security in a world with less than porous borders.

Watching Frank as he presented these lectures I got a sense of how he moves between differing claims. On the one hand compassion so animates him, a compassion as natural as his transparency; on the other hand, there's his admiration for law and its dependence on order, that sometimes, while working for the common good, might not yield as quickly or as compassionately as we or he would like. Still throughout it all, Frank leads us to think further, to find better solutions, to move spatially ahead along with the very people who most animate us by their needs.

In these pages there is a realism then, but it's a realism built on the first chapter where human dignity provides the foundation for the compassionate claims as well as the law and order that can meet those claims. Keeping these values together is the key.

Rightly then, Frank concludes the first chapter with these words:

> Working from the strength of our tradition and from the immediacy of our contact with the marginalised, we can contribute to the culture, public dialogue, and legal structures necessary for enhancing human dignity and public order for all.

For me these words are a worthy introduction to his thought and to this volume.

James F Keenan, SJ
Canisius Professor
(Former Gasson Professor, 2003–2005)

Introduction

Having Space and Thriving on Difference

In 2014–2015, I was the Gasson Professor at the Boston College Law School. This book contains three of my Gasson Lectures. I have always enjoyed the opportunity to spend time in the United States observing how people in a different society from mine deal with the contested issues of law, public policy, morality, and religion. It is often in the differences that we find the space for new thinking and fresh perspectives, regardless of our religious or political tradition. Having the time to think and write, away from my regular duties, I wanted to wrestle with some of the big unresolved public policy issues which call into question everything including our more traditional thinking on morality and religion—issues like physician-assisted suicide, and asylum at national borders.

Thomas Ignatius Gasson was born in 1859 to Anglican and Huguenot parents in England and migrated to the United States at the age of thirteen years after his mother had died and his father remarried. Becoming a Catholic in his new home country at age fifteen, he joined the Jesuits one year later. He was sent for theology studies to Austria. He then taught in various institutions elsewhere in the United States before being coming to Boston College in 1895, aged thirty-six. He became university president in 1907. When his term ended in 1914, he was sent to Georgetown University where he taught legal ethics. He spent his last six years living and working in Canada. During that time he taught at Loyola College in Montreal. He died in Montreal in 1930, aged seventy-one. His funeral cortege passed through the Boston College campus prior to his burial, honouring his contribution to the building of the new BC. It is therefore fitting that lectures in his name engage in some comparative analysis of states and societies such as the United States, Canada, Europe and the United Kingdom. In this twenty-first century, I am sure he would have no objection to the inclusion of Australia.

Like Gasson, I am a Jesuit priest. He was a professor of ethics and economics. I am a professor of law who has spent most of his Jesuit working life, other than study, engaged in the public square agitating issues of human rights and social justice. I have had the benefit every ten years to spend some time at a Jesuit university in the United States—in 1995 at Georgetown, and in 2005 and 2015 at Boston College. Preparing to return to my ministry in the public square in Australia, I have had cause once again to reflect on truth speaking to power, and more precisely, on religious truth speaking to and informing the exercise of political power in the public square of a pluralist society in a democratic state under the rule of law. I am now thirty years a priest and forty years a Jesuit, so I am probably settling into the role as best I ever will.

In the United States, almost any issue can be hotly contested in the public square and then litigated in the highest court. Only in the United States could there be threatened boycotts and litigation over whether a florist or a baker might decline the request to prepare an elaborate flower arrangement or a personalised wedding cake for a same sex marriage. Discussing the matter with a class at Boston College, I said that I had no problem with the bakery or the flower shop being required to sell bread and flowers in a non-discriminatory way. You either sell goods to everybody or to nobody. Gone are the days of having signs in shops: Catholics need not apply; or Blacks will not be served.

I then said I was happy to show deference to the artistic florist or religious baker who says: 'Doing a wedding arrangement is an expression of my artistic and/or religious understanding of what is being celebrated, and thus I choose not to agree to your request that I provide my artistic services for a professional fee at your gay wedding. I just wouldn't be able to put my heart in it, as I would need to do if I were to produce an arrangement of true excellence. I think it would be better for everyone if you approached the baker or florist around the corner (though admittedly I think they're not quite as artistic or expressive as I am), and I promise not to say a word to anyone. Have a great party! I don't want to cause you any offence, upset or embarrassment. I just wouldn't be able to bring myself to do it joyfully and passionately. I hope you understand.'

I told the class that I would prefer to live in a society where that was possible—maximising freedom for all, provided of course there was another florist or baker on hand, and provided there was no adverse public discrimination in the sale of bread or flowers. The students looked at me in stunned silence as if I were being Jesuitical or quaintly old-fashioned. I suspect some of them thought, 'He's not American. He just doesn't get it.' These sorts of exchanges assist our deliberation on difficult new social questions, requiring us to review our traditional thought patterns as well as our cultural and religious preconceptions.

I hope these lectures provide a fresh perspective and not just for Catholics and not just for Australians, though I happen to be an Australian Catholic priest. I also hope that these lectures can help persons of all faiths and none maintain what Pope John Paul II, when addressing the Italian Parliament, called 'a convinced and pondered trust in the heritage of virtues and values handed down by your forebears'[1]. In these lectures I have drawn much inspiration from Pope Francis who travelled to the island of Lampedusa to speak boldly and prophetically about the plight of asylum seekers coming across the Mediterranean Sea in search of new life. Before offering his blessing and casting a wreath on the waters, Francis asked, 'Who is responsible for the blood of these brothers and sisters of ours?' In these lectures, I seek to draw on my own religious tradition to answer that question to the satisfaction of persons of all faiths and none, and in the many precarious situations in which people find themselves, especially at the borders of life and of nation states.

---

1. See http://www.vatican.va/holy_father/john_paul_ii/speeches/2002/november/documents/hf_jp-ii_spe_20021114_italian-parliament_en.html.

Chapter 1

Human Dignity and Public Order

We live in societies in which notions of autonomy, individual human rights and non-discrimination are trumps. They are trumps even when players in the public square have given insufficient consideration to human dignity, the common good and the public interest. Often the cry is heard, 'The state should just butt out, and leave the individual to decide'; 'The church should just butt out and leave society free to make decisions about laws and policies regardless of the comprehensive world view of any particular group.' When is church intervention in public debate warranted? When is state intervention in an individual's life and in the social life of citizens warranted?

As one who dips back into political philosophy every decade or so, I am constantly bemused that there is an ever reducing prospect of academic consensus about the grounds on which the state might intervene with a person's autonomy. Any state interference with an individual requires justification.

Those of a Kantian bent will seek to formulate universal propositions which apply to all similarly situated individuals and cases. Those of a utilitarian bent will attempt a calculus of greatest happiness or greatest benefit. Those of a liberal bent will start by countenancing interference with liberty only for the sake of liberty, discounting anyone's comprehensive worldview. Some liberals will exclude any consideration of the possibility of law and policy being used to achieve some state of perfection counselled by a particular comprehensive worldview. Those who have followed the tortuous path of John Rawls and the debate between him and Jürgen Habermas will espouse a political liberalism which insists on a place for the diverse comprehensive world views of citizens provided only that those views can be translated into positions and actions comprehensible and endorsable by others who do not hold the same comprehensive world view. While espousing the need for public reason by judges and legislators, they will ultimately concede that citizens and collectives like churches can participate in the background culture or cultures bringing the fullness of their comprehensive world views to bear on the matter at hand while insisting that in due course they be able to translate their aspirations giving 'properly public reasons to support the principles and policies (their) comprehensive doctrine is said to support'[1].

No matter which side of the mountain we scale on the way to the summit of political justification, we know that we live in a cultural milieu in which interference with the autonomous action of the self-determining citizen requires a threefold assessment: does this interference respect all human rights? Is this interference conducted in a non-discriminatory way? Does this interference with individual autonomy contribute to some greater good, to greater happiness, or to some greater liberty for all?

In an article entitled 'Two-way Translation: The Ethics of Engaging with Religious Contributions in Public Deliberation', Jeremy Waldron joins issue with John Rawls' assertion that the responsibility falls on the religious speaker rather than the secular listener to translate his propositions and his moral passion into language comprehensible to those who profess nothing more than the tenets of public reason. He quotes Jürgen Habermas who insists that any 'requirement of translation must be conceived as a cooperative task in which the nonreligious citizens must likewise participate.' Discourse in the public square is a two-way street.

There is a place for church leaders drawing on their religious tradition trying to call political leaders and the public back to values, policies and laws which resonate more with the tenets of religious faith. Following Habermas, Waldron states:

> It is not only speakers who bear a burden of civility; the audience does too. The speaker must strain to convey his points in ways that will communicate as much of their content as he can to those who do not share his faith or the

---

1. John Rawls, The Idea of Public Reason in *The Law of Peoples* (Harvard: Harvard University Press, 1999), 144.

biblical or theological resources he is drawing on. But the listener has a similar responsibility. He must strain to listen and try to understand what is being said, and, if necessary, draw on resources in his own background (even aspects of his background that he has repudiated) or resources in the culture that he has access to, to get a bearing on what is being said, and what is being argued.

Certainly, it is not appropriate—it is not civil—for secular citizens to strain not to understand what is being said to publicly burnish their own credentials as non-believers. It is not appropriate for them to block out or refuse to employ available resources for making sense of what is said, because of their own resolve to purge religion from their lives. Or rather, a person can do that; people do not have the obligation to listen to and grapple with everything that is said in public discourse. But then, if they do turn a deaf ear, for whatever reason, to some of what is being said, they can hardly complain about the incivility of the speaker.[2]

The three-fold assessment of rights, discrimination and the common good must be conducted through dialogue in which there is sufficient trust for any participant to question the cultural norms of the day. The dialogue needs to occur in the diverse *fora* provided by the constitutional arrangements of the particular nation state. But it can also occur in conversations amongst citizens everywhere from the airwaves to the kitchen table.

I am one of those non-Americans who delights at a distance in the blind faith which is placed in the United States constitutional role of federal judges with life appointments charged to provide the ultimate determination on all manner of contested social/moral questions from same sex marriage, to physician-assisted suicide, and to the acceptable parameters of the death penalty. I live in one of those societies where we entrust less of these tasks to the judges (who must retire at seventy anyway) and more to our elected politicians. We Australians usually come up with the same answer and at about the same time, though happily we regard the death penalty as the barbarous hangover of a

---

2. Jeremy Waldron, 'Two-way Translation: The Ethics of Engaging with Religious Contributions in Public Deliberation', (2012) 63 M*ercer Law Review* 845 at 863–4.

bygone era, especially when it can be imposed by state elected judges overriding juries who have opted for life imprisonment.

Coming from a country with such a different constitutional architecture, I wonder whether the interminable American debate about such practical questions as 'abortion, military policy or economic justice' is 'because the reigning categories of public discourse are inadequate to deal with them' as David Hollenbach suggests.[3] Undoubtedly that is one of the reasons. But to an outsider it is not axiomatic that the United States Supreme Court give the last word on abortion but not on military policy or economic justice. I have no doubt that a society like mine benefits from the fine grained agitation which lawyers and judges apply through the devices of due process and equal protection, mitigated by varying degrees of scrutiny and unreviewable, inscrutable decisions whether and when to grant *cert*. It may be that societies like Australia with different constitutional architecture provide a readier resolution of the interminable debate when an issue like abortion is, like military policy or economic justice, left to elected legislators rather than unelected judges. The losers are more likely to wear the result as part the price of living in a democratic society.

After my first visit to the United States in 1995, I wrote a book *Legislating Liberty* in which I confessed delight to live in a nation state where the elected politicians rather than the unelected judges made the decision about the legality of abortion. The abortion rates are the same in each country. But the issue remains much more divisive in the United States, precisely because unelected judges purported to legislate for all. The purpose served by the *amicus* brief in the United States is fulfilled by the submission to a parliamentary committee in Australia. What is missing in Australia is the jurisprudence of equal protection, due process, and diverse levels of scrutiny. But the philosophical discussion about the limits of, and rationale for, state interference is the same. This is not an argument for change in the United States, but neither is it an argument for change in Australia. With our own distinctive constitutional arrangements in place we seem to get by. As ever, there is the prospect that learning could be a two-way street.

---

3. David Hollenbach, *The Global Face of Public Faith* (Georgetown: Georgetown University Press, 2003), 120.

The United States Supreme Court has now legislated for universal recognition of same sex marriage. Within the next year or two, the Australian parliament will legislate for it. I predict the result will be more universally accepted in Australia because everyone, including the losers in the debate, will concede that they have had the opportunity to put their case, they have been heard, and all points of view will have been agitated in the chamber of public deliberation—the Parliament. In the United States, the losers will be left thinking that a legal elite has pushed the reform at a pace beyond the public sentiment of those elected to office to represent the people.

Given developments in countries like Ireland and the United States, I have accepted the inevitability that civil marriage in Australia will be redefined to include same sex couples. Given the increasing number of children being brought up by same sex couples, I think it is a good thing that the state take away any social stigma against same sex parents. Given the ageing population, I think the state has an interest in recognising and protecting long term relationships of same sex couples who care for each other. It is one thing for the civil law to recognise same sex unions as marriages. It is another thing to require all persons, regardless of their religious beliefs, to treat same sex couples even in the life and activities of the Church as if they were married in the eyes of the Church. At the moment, some religious institutions restrict facilities such as shared accommodation on a church site to married couples. Would the maintenance of that restriction in future be judged discriminatory and unlawful? Some religious schools limit employment to teachers who follow the church teaching on sexual relations. Would the exclusion of a homosexual person be prohibited once they had entered into a state recognised same sex marriage? Faith based adoption agencies tend to have a preference for placing a child who is not related to any prospective adoptive parent with a family unit including an adult male and an adult female. Would that now be judged discriminatory? In the future, religious groups are sure to have an interest in asserting that reproductive technology should be limited so that any child will be assured a known biological mother and a known biological father. Will that be judged bigoted discrimination? I hope not. But I do think these issues should be squarely on the table now. The unfortunate effect of the United States Supreme Court decision is that all these issues have been put off to another day without discussion and with the imputation that they are the concerns only of bigots or old-fashioned religious zealots. Even bakers, florists and marriage counselors are told that they need to provide their services for same sex marriages. Why not just go and find another florist, baker or counselor? Some of us support the state recognition of both same sex marriage AND religious freedom exercised in speech, actions and institutional arrangements. Sadly many who advocate same sex marriage have no time for those of us who espouse religious freedom as well.

Once the United States Supreme Court and the Australian parliament have dealt with same sex marriage, they will inevitably return to the issue of euthanasia and physician-assisted suicide. Our societies have a way of throwing up the same moral issues at about the same time seeking resolution through courts or parliaments.

Religious freedom is always a contested issue in these debates. The Catholic Church made a significant turnaround on this issue at the second Vatican Council. The Vatican Council's Declaration on Religious Freedom (*Dignitatis Humanae*) espoused the right of religious freedom, while stating that the exercise of the right was subject to certain regulatory norms, having regard to the rights of others, the need to deal with others in justice and civility, the need to settle peacefully any conflict of rights, and the need for public peace, good order and the guardianship of public morality.

Living and working in societies where there is no philosophical agreement about the basis for, or the limits of, state power interfering with personal autonomy, and being members of faith communities and churches without any theological consensus about the basis of human rights and human dignity (inherent or attributed), how can we authentically and usefully contribute to the development of laws and public policies which enhance human flourishing, and perhaps even counsel a social striving for perfection? This is a question which confronts all religious leaders in a pluralistic democratic society. It may be an even more pressing question for the citizen of faith who occupies a position of public trust, whether as legislator, judge or administrator. What can we do? What should we do? What should we forbear from doing, regardless of our personal convictions, when discharging that public trust? What can we learn from those in countries with diverse constitutional arrangements (such as the

United States, Canada, the United Kingdom, Australia, and the European Union) about how best to resolve disputes about law and policy relating to contested moral questions? How can the human rights actor best speak out for those suffering, whilst maintaining the agency of those suffering?

Those of us who profess to be Christian, living behind secure national borders buttressed by wealth and the rule of law being shared only by the citizenry, have been wrestling with the gospel imperatives of justice and compassion expressed in the parables of Jesus such as the parable of the Good Samaritan. The Oxford academic John Finnis reminds us that 'neither atheism nor radical agnosticism is entitled to be treated as the 'default' position in public reason, deliberation and decisions. Those who say or assume that there is a default position and that it is secular in those senses (atheism or agnosticism about atheism) owe us an argument that engages with and defeats the best arguments for divine causality.'[4] Though it might be prudent and strategic to suggest that religious accommodationists carry the onus of persuasion in a public square with a secularist prejudice, might there not be a case for arguing that the representatives of the more populist, majoritarian mindset in the public square need to be more accommodating of religious views?

Finnis, a Catholic but making a point equally applicable to all faith communities, says, 'Outside the Church, it is widely assumed and asserted that any proposition which the Catholic Church in fact proposes for acceptance is, by virtue of that fact, a "religious" (not a philosophical, scientific, or rationally grounded and compelling proposition), and is a proposition which Catholics hold only as a matter of faith and therefore cannot be authentically willing to defend as a matter of natural reason.'[5] For Finnis, much of what John Rawls in his *Political Liberalism* describes as public reason can be equated with natural reason. Whereas Rawls would rely on an overlapping consensus not wanting to press for objective reality of right and wrong, Finnis would contest that the only content of an overlapping consensus would be that which can be objectively known through natural reason.

---

4. John Finnis, *Religion and Public Reasons* (Oxford: Oxford University Press, 2011), 45.
5. Finnis, *Religion and Public Reasons*, 114–5.

Discourse in the public square is a two-way street. Thus, for example, there is a place for Pope Francis at Lampedusa to be prophetically declaiming the moral turpitude of present European state practices in relation to the rescue of asylum seekers in the Mediterranean Sea. There is a place for the Australian Catholic bishops to be prophetically declaiming the moral turpitude of present state practices towards asylum seekers on Christmas Island, Nauru and Manus Island. There is a place for those like Cardinal O'Malley celebrating Mass at the Mexican border and handing communion to congregation members through the iron border fence. There is a place for church leaders drawing on their religious tradition trying to call political leaders and the public back to values, policies and laws which resonate more with the tenets of religious faith.

The migration and asylum debate is one debate in which the voice of community leaders, and not just international lawyers, needs to be heeded and in which we need to have due regard for political deliberation. It is one of those debates requiring an attentiveness to all the still, small voices of conscience. Often nowadays the best amplifiers of that voice are not the religious leaders but the poets, novelists and folk singers. In Australia, one of our finest novelists Tim Winton made a rare appearance on the public stage on Palm Sunday 2015, dissenting from Australia's refugee policy. Conceding that he was 'no expert, no politician', and expressing no envy of 'those who make the decisions in these matters, those who've sought and gained the power to make decisions in this matter', he declared, 'But I know when something's wrong. And what my country is doing is wrong.'[6] He lamented:

> We're losing our way. We have hardened our hearts. I fear we have devalued the currency of mercy. Children have asked for bread and we gave them stones. So turn back. I beg you. For the children's sake. For the sake of this nation's spirit. Raise us back up to our best selves. Turn back while there's still time.

As we witness in the United States, the migration and asylum debate can be properly conducted only with institutional safeguards, those checks and balances ensuring appropriate consideration of the

---

6. See http://www.watoday.com.au/comment/tim-wintons-palm-sunday-plea-start-the-soulsearching-australia-20150329-1ma5so.html.

balance between the public interest and the dignity of every person, including the person presenting at the national border in flight from persecution. This requires adequate supervision by the domestic courts. It requires strong political virtue in national leaders, opinion makers and public advocates. It requires a honed ethical inquiry into the ends to be achieved, given the vast numbers of people seeking protection and the heightened need to secure national borders. For example, it is not an ethical irrelevance that for every person who gains protection at the border in Australia, that is one less place available in the annual immigration intake for a person in great humanitarian need who does not have the resources to get themselves to the border.

In what circumstances are we entitled to turn away the person on our doorstep so that we might put out the welcome mat to the person in greater need on the other side of the world? In what circumstances are we entitled to welcome the person on our doorstep, absolving ourselves from responsibility for the person in greater need in a remote refugee camp where the human rights violations are horrendous? It is facile to suggest that there is some simple mathematical answer to these political and ethical quandaries.

In his inaugural lecture at Oxford, Professor Waldron spoke about *political* political theory and the need to be 'focusing on issues of institutions as well as the ends, aims, and ideals of politics, like justice'. He observed:

> The deliberative and deliberate processes of a free society slow things down; their articulated and articulate structures stretch things out; they cost money for salaries and furniture and buildings; they provide an irritating place for the raising of inconvenient questions; at their best they respect the dignity of the poorest he or the poorest she that is in England by providing a place for their petitions to be heard. The political institutions of a free society sometimes even require the government to retire from the field defeated, when its victory, in some courtroom or legislative battle, was supposed by political insiders to be a foregone conclusion. I think all of this is to be valued and cherished.[7]

---

7. Jeremy Waldron, '*Political* Political Theory: An Inaugural lecture', in *The Journal of Political Philosophy*, 21 (2013): 1, 23.

Waldron is adamant that students of politics need to study both institutions and the character of those who inhabit them: 'They should understand something of political virtue and the demands that the requirements of good government make on the character of those who take on responsibility for public affairs'. We need to improve both if we are to get better ethical outcomes for laws and policies affecting those who present at our borders seeking protection whether from persecution, torture, cruel or inhuman treatment.

Just as the conscientious citizen living in a society lacking an intellectual consensus for state intervention in personal life decisions needs to resolve which side of the mountain to scale rather than being paralysed back at the base camp of daily social life, so too the citizen with a religious perspective needs to settle on a mode of theological argument about the basis for political action and constitutional engagement in the life of the state consistent with the citizen's religious faith.

Christians in the Catholic tradition will want to give considerable weight to the role of tradition, authority, ritual and community. One of the liberating and confusing aspects of Francis's papacy is just how fungible tradition and authority are when one takes seriously the experience and reflection on experience by members of the church community. There is a need to distinguish the pope's dogmatic, pastoral, and pedagogical utterances and actions. One of the delights of Pope Francis's approach is the primacy he gives to pastoral solicitude, leaving aside the insistence on repeated dogmatic utterances which maintain or develop the corpus of papal teaching on all manner of contested issues.

Take for example the approach of Pope Francis to the issue of birth control. His reaffirmation of the key teaching of Paul VI's *Humanae Vitae* that 'each and every marital act must of necessity retain its intrinsic relationship to the procreation of human life', together with his press conference urging, in light of the case of a woman confronting her eighth birth by caesarean section, that there is no need for good Catholic women to breed like rabbits highlights that a mechanical application of papal directives no longer coheres for the faithful, let alone for their fellow-citizens who are outside the faith community. In fact it no longer coheres even for the members of the hierarchy who, though being required to affirm the teaching prior to their elevation to the episcopacy, know that it is incomprehensible to many believers of good faith in the living of their daily lives. Instead of simply restating the legal prohibition enunciated by Paul VI, Francis has now said:

> [The] key word is the one the Church always uses all the time and even I use it: it is responsible parenthood. How do we do this? With dialogue. Each person with his pastor seeks how to do that responsible parenthood.
>
> That example I mentioned shortly before about that woman who was expecting her eighth (child) and already had seven who were born with caesareans. That is an irresponsibility (That woman might say) 'no but I trust in God'. But God gives you methods to be responsible. Some think that, excuse me if I use that word, that in order to be good Catholics we have to be like rabbits. No. Responsible parenthood! This is clear and that is why in the church there are marriage groups, there are experts in this matter, there are pastors, one can seek and I know so many, many ways out that are licit and that have helped this.[8]

What is essential is the dialogue which calls everyone to the table, taking seriously the experience and reflection on experience of the individual. If this can be done by the pope in relation to such a clearly narrowly articulated and constantly contested papal teaching as that against artificial contraception, it can be done by anyone in relation to any contested moral issue. If he knows 'so many, many ways out that are licit', then it is time to abandon the restrictive teaching of Paul VI which indicated only two licit ways out—abstinence and sexual relations during the assured non-fertile period.

The forty-seven year impasse over *Humanae Vitae* provides one note of liberation. Not even the pope any longer thinks that the matter can be resolved simply by applying the teaching of *Humanae Vitae* as a legal directive. The pope has spoken of the need for dialogue. That is the process. And he has spoken of the need for responsible parenthood. That is the outcome. It is done by maintaining a convinced and pondered trust in the heritage of virtues and values handed down

---

8. See Transcript of Pope Francis's press conference on plane from Manila, 19 January 2015 at http://americamagazine.org/content/dispatches/full-transcript-popes-press-conference-flight-manila.

to us, not by applying a legal prohibition which unnecessarily restricts the means for achieving responsible parenthood.

When considering the relationship between the state and the individual, it is usual nowadays to invoke the language of human rights. Everyone agrees that rights can be limited by rights. My right to free speech is limited by your right to reputation. My right to swing my arm is limited by your right to bodily integrity. For some, the state ought to maximally recognise individual rights provided only that it acts in a non-discriminatory way towards persons, or at least towards citizens (often making an exception for those who are not citizens seeking access or residence), or at least towards self-determining citizens (often making an exception for those at either end of the life cycle or for those unable to help themselves). But the more the exceptions or limitations are considered, the more necessary it is to accommodate notions such as the common good, public morality, the public interest or public order.

The application of the rule of law ensures greater universalism and equality of application of the law. Like cases are treated similarly. Like persons are treated similarly. There are some things we do not do to anybody. There are some actions by the state which we do not authorise upon persons. This gives rise to the notion of human dignity. As Immanuel Kant says, 'In the kingdom of ends everything has either a *price* or a *dignity*. What has a price can be replaced by something else as its *equivalent*; what on the other hand is above all price and therefore admits of no equivalent has a dignity.' The individual human being has a dignity which is to be respected even if the person is to be punished or deprived of liberty. Law, like the notion of human dignity, takes seriously equality and liberty enjoyed universally. The rule of law ensures that we can set the contours for everyone's dignity to be respected.

When it comes to public deliberation, the Church needs to have the humility to admit its slowness sometimes to keep pace with critical moral reflection. Society needs to have the humility to admit that usually not every conceivable case is on the table when developments occur in law and policy. What about when we just don't know the likely outcome? The voice of the Church is to be heard asking, 'Have we considered all possible cases?' 'Are we cognizant of all the consequences of this course of action?' If not, are we warranted in legislating in this way, potentially to the detriment of a class of persons not represented here at the table of deliberation. I have been helped by Kent Greenawalt's phrase: the borderlines of status. We need to look to those on the borders of life: the refugees and asylum seekers, the indigenous people in our post-colonial societies, the unborn and the dying; those with a disability. The Church in the public square can play the role of placing those at the margins at the centre of our deliberations.

I have the good fortune of having a father who is an accomplished lawyer (he was Chief Justice of Australia). When coming to Boston College I asked him what I should be thinking about while here pondering the role of the priest in the public square. He responded:

> To create, by example, by precept and by proclamation, the social conditions that facilitate the dignified treatment of every person in order to allow each person to live in dignity. But more, by the same means, to explain in terms comprehensible to the contemporary individual, the significance of God's love and the life God has intended for human kind and to demonstrate the vastly enhanced significance of dignity to the believing individual and the moral unacceptability of undignified treatment because it interferes with the divine plan for human kind.

I was assisted by a few observations by Martin O'Malley, retiring governor of Maryland at the 2015 Society of Christian Ethics Conference. He told us that 'living systems find stability through diversity. Ideologues believe it's done through the opposite.' He suggested that when drawing the line between private and public morality, one needed discernment and dialogue. From his experience, he claimed that 'elected leaders make themselves vulnerable by coming to the centre of the conversation on race, justice and crime', needing to admit their own fears. When contemplating the great economic challenges before us, he put the stark proposition that a society could be made more competitive by making the middle class more vulnerable. In this era of the 24-hour news media cycle he admitted the need for us to return 'to making the better choices we have made over the long term'. He told us, 'In the absence of a clear affirmative economic theory, people revert to fear and anger which wins elections but does not build a country.'

When O'Malley as governor proposed legislation for the recognition of same sex marriage, he received a strong, critical letter from his Catholic bishop. He took time to respond, suggesting that 'on this bridge between the sacred and secular', one needs to respond 'without anger or resentment'. Harking back to the abortion debate, he suggested that 'progress is best achieved by relying on the conscience of women rather than the coercive power of the state.' Since O'Malley spoke, the United States Supreme Court by the narrowest of margins has determined that same sex couples have a constitutional right to marry.

As a respectful foreign observer, I think it is regrettable that the Supreme Court took it upon itself to discover a definitive answer in the silent Constitution on this contested social question, because there can be no doubt that the democratic process was taking United States society in only one direction on the issue. The court by intervening and deciding the issue unilaterally has reduced the prospects of community acceptance and of community compromise about the freedom of religious practice of those who cannot embrace same sex marriage for religious reasons. Justice Alito is right when he assumes 'that those who cling to old beliefs will be able to whisper their thoughts in the recesses of their homes, but if they repeat those views in public, they will risk being labelled as bigots and treated as such by governments, employers, and schools'[9].

The majority overlooked the very fine *amicus* brief submitted by four of the United States's leading scholars on freedom of religion who were strong supporters of same sex marriage while at the same time pointing out:

> If this Court holds that same-sex marriage is constitutionally required, it must take responsibility for the resulting issues of religious liberty, because a constitutional decision will largely displace legislative efforts to address the issue. States that have enacted same-sex civil marriage by legislation have generally included provisions to protect religious liberty. But where marriage equality has arrived by judicial decision, religious liberty has not been protected. When courts find a constitutional right to same-sex civil marriage, those who would add religious liberty provisions to a marriage bill are

---

9. *Obergefell v. Hodges* 576 U. S. ____ (2015) at p 7 (Justice Alito).

> deprived of a legislative vehicle and deprived of bargaining leverage. Legislative bargaining is critical to protecting religious liberty in the growing number of states where religious objections to same-sex marriage have become unpopular. A constitutional decision by this Court will end legislative efforts to protect religious liberty as part of legislation enacting marriage equality. If the Court protects same-sex marriage, it must also protect religious liberty with respect to marriage.[10]

There will be years of litigation now about the right of religious bodies to restrict services only to couples who marry in accordance with the institution's religious creed. It will all be nasty and hard fought.

Unfortunately, the president of the United States Catholic Bishops Conference (USCCB), Archbishop Joseph E Kurtz of Louisville, Kentucky, adopted a very unconciliatory tone in his official response to the judgment, displaying absolutely no pastoral sensitivity to same sex couples and their supporters rejoicing in the decision. He claimed:

> Just as *Roe v. Wade* did not settle the question of abortion over forty years ago, *Obergefell v. Hodges* does not settle the question of marriage today. Neither decision is rooted in the truth, and as a result, both will eventually fail. Today the Court is wrong again. It is profoundly immoral and unjust for the government to declare that two people of the same sex can constitute a marriage . . . Mandating marriage redefinition across the country is a tragic error that harms the common good and most vulnerable among us, especially children. The law has a duty to support every child's basic right to be raised, where possible, by his or her married mother and father in a stable home.[11]

---

10. Brief of *Obergefell v. Hodges*, Amicus Brief Of Douglas Laycock, Thomas C Berg, David Blankenhorn, Marie A Failinger, and Edward Mcglynn Gaffney, As Amici Curiae in Support of Petitioners, 6 March 2015, 2–3.
11. Joseph E Kurtz, News Release, United States Conference of Catholic Bishops, 26 June 2015.

The argument about children needs to be much more nuanced nowadays, especially given the observation by Justice Kennedy: 'As all parties agree, many same-sex couples provide loving and nurturing homes to their children, whether biological or adopted. And hundreds of thousands of children are presently being raised by such couples.'[12] These hundreds of thousands of children did not warrant even a mention by the archbishop.

The new Archbishop of Chicago Blase Cupich, Pope Francis's 'captain's pick', was in Rome to receive the pallium when the court announced its decision. He took a far more conciliatory and pastoral approach than the president of the USCCB, observing:

> It is important to note that the Catholic Church has an abiding concern for the dignity of gay persons. In fact, the *Catechism of the Catholic Church* says: 'They must be accepted with respect, compassion, and sensitivity. Every sign of unjust discrimination in their regard should be avoided.' This respect must be real, not rhetorical, and ever reflective of the Church's commitment to accompanying all people. For this reason, the Church must extend support to all families, no matter their circumstances, recognizing that we are all relatives, journeying through life under the careful watch of a loving God.[13]

Same sex marriage is or soon will be a legal reality in all well educated, developed societies in the foreseeable future. It is imperative that the Church continue to advocate the ideal of sacramental marriage for a man and a woman who are believers wanting to commit themselves to each other before God open to the bearing and nurturing of each other's children according to the law of Christ and His Church. It is appropriate that the Church continue to espouse the ideal that children be nurtured in a family unit by their known biological mother and known biological father, while extending pastoral solicitude to all families and to all children, including the hundreds of thousands who are already being raised by same sex couples. Our bishops need to accept that the contours of civil marriage have not been identical with the attributes of sacramental marriage for a very long time. Perhaps

---

12. *Obergefell v. Hodges* 576 US ____ (2015) at p 15 (Justice Kennedy).
13. Statement of Blase J Cupich, 28 June 2015.

part the episcopal fear is that even those married in Church have little understanding of the difference between the two institutions, and many of the clergy are ill-equipped to explain the difference.

Whatever one's misgivings about Justice Kennedy's judicial technique in writing for the five majority justices, there can be no faulting his pastoral sensitivity to those same sex couples who have felt alienated and marginalised for too long. Our bishops would do well to replicate the pastoral tone at the conclusion of his majority judgment:

> No union is more profound than marriage, for it embodies the highest ideals of love, fidelity, devotion, sacrifice, and family. In forming a marital union, two people become something greater than once they were. As some of the petitioners in these cases demonstrate, marriage embodies a love that may endure even past death. It would misunderstand these men and women to say they disrespect the idea of marriage. Their plea is that they do respect it so deeply that they seek to find its fulfilment for themselves. Their hope is not to be condemned to live in loneliness, excluded from one of civilisation's oldest institutions.[14]

As Pope Francis said on that airplane: 'Who am I to judge?' I agree with the late Mario Cuomo when he said at Notre Dame: 'I'm convinced we will all benefit if suspicion is replaced by discussion, innuendo by dialogue; if the emphasis in our debate turns from a search for talismanic criteria and neat but simplistic answers to an honest—more intelligent—attempt at describing the role religion has in our public affairs, and the limits placed on that role.'[15] Discussion and dialogue are the key. That's been the signature contribution of Pope Francis. At Notre Dame, Cuomo quoted his own local bishop Joseph Sullivan who said:

> The major problem the Church has is internal. How do we teach? As much as I think we're responsible for advocating public policy issues, our primary responsibility is to teach our

---

14. *Obergefell v. Hodges* 576 U. S. ____ (2015) at p 28 (Justice Kennedy).
15. Mario Cuomo, 'Religious Belief and Public Morality: A Catholic Governor's Perspective', Remarks Delivered at Notre Dame University, 13 September 1984, at <http://archives.nd.edu/research/texts/cuomo.htm>.

own people. We haven't done that. We're asking politicians to do what we haven't done effectively ourselves.

As Cuomo said, 'Better than any law or rule or threat of punishment would be the moving strength of our own good example, demonstrating our lack of hypocrisy, proving the beauty and worth of our instruction.' I do not think Pope Francis would have any trouble with that suggestion.

The overly prescriptive approach of Pope John Paul II culminating in his encyclicals *Evangelium Vitae* and *Veritatis Splendor* have given way to the more accommodating approaches of Benedict and Francis. I include Benedict because he insisted on the link between faith and reason, while distinguishing the distinctive roles of the church and state, thus providing the readier distinction, as well as the link, between the language and thinking of the background culture and the language and thinking appropriate to the public square, namely public reason. And Francis who without rewriting past papal and curial texts about intrinsic disorder and intrinsic evil, asks, 'Who am I to judge?', urging that there are many licit ways. In *Deus Caritas Est*, Benedict enunciated this view in 2005:

> The Church's social teaching argues on the basis of reason and natural law, namely, on the basis of what is in accord with the nature of every human being. It recognizes that it is not the Church's responsibility to make this teaching prevail in political life. Rather, the Church wishes to help form consciences in political life and to stimulate greater insight into the authentic requirements of justice as well as greater readiness to act accordingly, even when this might involve conflict with situations of personal interest. Building a just social and civil order, wherein each person receives what is his or her due, is an essential task which every generation must take up anew. As a political task, this cannot be the Church's immediate responsibility. Yet, since it is also a most important human responsibility, the Church is duty-bound to offer, through the purification of reason and through ethical formation, her own specific contribution towards understanding the requirements of justice and achieving them politically.
>
> The Church cannot and must not take upon herself the political battle to bring about the most just society possible.

> She cannot and must not replace the State. Yet at the same time she cannot and must not remain on the sidelines in the fight for justice. She has to play her part through rational argument and she has to reawaken the spiritual energy without which justice, which always demands sacrifice, cannot prevail and prosper. A just society must be the achievement of politics, not of the Church. Yet the promotion of justice through efforts to bring about openness of mind and will to the demands of the common good is something which concerns the Church deeply.[16]

As Church we have a role in the public square in helping to shape the values of our political leaders, in critiquing the structures of our political institutions, and in clarifying the ends of our society including justice and compassion for all, bringing to bear what Benedict calls the purification of reason. This can be done in the public square of the pluralistic democratic society by a church like the Catholic Church only if there be some restored credibility about justice and transparency within the Church, the shortcomings of which have been so highlighted by the child sexual abuse crisis, and if there be continued public admission of church shortcomings abandoning any 'holier than thou' approach.

The voice of conscience missions the believer not just for service in the Church but most especially for service in the world, not just with commitment to justice in the Church but most especially to justice in the world. This cannot be done without a commitment to laws and policies which do justice, protecting the weak and vulnerable. It is a call to take an intelligent, informed stand in solidarity. In his encyclical *Laudato Si'*, Pope Francis calls us to consider the tragic effects of environmental degradation especially on the lives of the world's poorest. He says:

> The problem is that we still lack the culture needed to confront this crisis. We lack leadership capable of striking out on new paths and meeting the needs of the present with concern for all and without prejudice towards coming generations. The establishment of a legal framework which can set clear boundaries and ensure the protection of ecosystems has

---

16. Pope Benedict XVI, *Deus Caritas Est*, #28.

become indispensable, otherwise the new power structures based on the techno-economic paradigm may overwhelm not only our politics but also freedom and justice.[17]

Developing the culture, the leadership, and the legal framework. These are the challenges to those of us who want to be intelligent believers responding to the call of the Spirit. It is heartening to note the pope's humility born of true consultation with bishops' conferences (17 of which are quoted directly in the encyclical) and detailed meetings with experts including scientists, economists and political scientists as well as philosophers and theologians. Having noted, 'There are certain environmental issues where it is not easy to achieve a broad consensus', he concedes that 'the Church does not presume to settle scientific questions or to replace politics. But I want to encourage an honest and open debate, so that particular interests or ideologies will not prejudice the common good'.[18] I suspect Pope Francis had some of our Jesuit alumni in mind when he wrote in his encyclical *Laudato Si'*:

> A politics concerned with immediate results, supported by consumerist sectors of the population, is driven to produce short-term growth. In response to electoral interests, governments are reluctant to upset the public with measures which could affect the level of consumption or create risks for foreign investment. The myopia of power politics delays the inclusion of a far-sighted environmental agenda within the overall agenda of governments. Thus we forget that 'time is greater than space', that we are always more effective when we generate processes rather than holding on to positions of power. True statecraft is manifest when, in difficult times, we uphold high principles and think of the long-term common good. Political powers do not find it easy to assume this duty in the work of nation-building.[19]

Five years ago in Mexico, Fr General Adolfo Nicolas put three major challenges to Jesuit university teachers in response to what he called the pervasive 'globalisation of superficiality' by which we can be

---

17. Pope Francis, *Laudato Si'*, #53.
18. Pope Francis, *Laudato Si'*, #188.
19. Pope Francis, *Laudato Si'*, #178.

'overwhelmed with such a dizzying pluralism of choices and values and beliefs and visions of life, then one can so easily slip into the lazy superficiality of relativism or mere tolerance of others and their views, rather than engaging in the hard work of forming communities of dialogue in the search of truth and understanding'. Fr Nicolas said:

> First, in response to the globalisation of superficiality, I suggest that we need to study the emerging cultural world of our students more deeply and find creative ways of promoting depth of thought and imagination, a depth that is transformative of the person. Second, in order to maximise the potentials of new possibilities of communication and cooperation, I urge the Jesuit universities to work towards operational international networks that will address important issues touching faith, justice, and ecology that challenge us across countries and continents. Finally, to counter the inequality of knowledge distribution, I encourage a search for creative ways of sharing the fruits of research with the excluded; and in response to the global spread of secularism and fundamentalism, I invite Jesuit universities to a renewed commitment to the Jesuit tradition of learned ministry which mediates between faith and culture.[20]

We Jesuits are now preparing for the 36th General Congregation of the Jesuits. And we are buoyed up by the leadership of our Jesuit Pope Francis who embodies so much of what we espouse and who challenges us to respond with full hearts, applied minds, and willing hands. Remember how Pope Francis ended his address to the journalists in Rome on the day after his election when he gave a blessing with a difference. He said:

> I told you I was cordially imparting my blessing. Since many of you are not members of the Catholic Church, and others are not believers, I cordially give this blessing silently, to each of

---

20. Adolfo Nicolas, 'Depth, Universality, And Learned Ministry: Challenges to Jesuit Higher Education Today', Address to the 'Networking Jesuit Higher Education: Shaping the Future for a Humane, Just, Sustainable Globe' Conference, Mexico City, 22 April 2010 at < http://www.scu.edu/scm/winter2010/shapingthefuture.cfm>.

you, respecting the conscience of each, but in the knowledge that each of you is a child of God. May God bless you![21]

Now that is what I call a real blessing for anybody and everybody—and not a word of Vaticanese. Respect for the conscience of every person, regardless of their religious beliefs; silence in the face of difference; affirmation of the dignity and blessedness of every person; offering, not coercing; suggesting, not dictating; leaving room for gracious acceptance. These are all good pointers for us members of the Jesuit Higher Education Network holding the treasure of the Ignatian tradition, Roman authority and Catholic ritual in trust for all people of good will, including all our staff and students, as we discern how best to make a home for God in our lives and in our world, assured that the Spirit of God has made her home with us.

Something crystallised for me at the splendid Sydney Opera House soon after the election of Francis when I appeared on stage with the British philosopher AC Grayling, author of *The God Argument*, and Sean Faircloth, the United States director of one of the Dawkins Institutes passionately committed to atheism. We were there to discuss their certainty about the absurdity of religious faith. Mr Faircloth raised what had already become a hoary old chestnut, the failure of Pope Francis when provincial of the Jesuits in Argentina during the Dirty Wars to adequately defend his fellow Jesuits who were detained and tortured by unscrupulous soldiers. Being a Jesuit, I thought I was peculiarly well situated to respond. I confess to having got a little carried away. I exclaimed: Yes, how much better it would have been if there had been just one secular, humanist, atheist philosopher who had stood up in the city square in Buenos Aires and shouted, 'Stop it!' The military junta would have collectively come to their senses, stopped it, and Argentinians would have lived happily ever after. The luxury for such philosophers is that they never have to get their hands dirty and they think that religious people who do are hypocrites unless of course they take the course of martyrdom. As believers, we are able to hold together ideals and reality, commitment and forgiveness.

---

21. Pope Francis, Address to Members of Communications Media, 16 March 2013, at <http://w2.vatican.va/content/francesco/en/speeches/2013/march/documents/papa-francesco_20130316_rappresentanti-media.html>.

In November 2014, the Boston College university community marked the 25th anniversary of the assassination of the six Jesuits, their housekeeper and her daughter at the Universidad Centroamerica (UCA) in El Salvador during their dreadful civil war. The American poet Carolyn Forché who spent years in El Salvador listening to the horrific stories addressed us. She spoke about 'A Poet's Journey from El Salvador to 2014: Witness in the Light of Conscience'. She knew Fr Ignacio Ellacuria SJ, the rector of UCA who was the main target of the assassins. He taught her that 'each moment of our life shapes the whole of our life, and that we are not always responsible for what befalls us but we are certainly responsible for our response'. He spoke of the capacity to meet the moment beautifully, and in a manner that honours our deepest human aspirations.

She was a friend of the late, now canonised, Archbishop Oscar Romero. She was with him the week before he was assassinated in March 1980. This is how she told the story:

> I met with Monsignor in the kitchen of the convent of the Carmelite Missionary Sisters, where he told me gently that it was time for me to go home, as the situation had become too dangerous, and I was more needed in the United States, in the work of helping Americans to understand the struggle for justice. But I begged him to leave, as his was the first name on the death squads' lists. He seemed so calm that afternoon, tapping his fingers on the Bible he carried with him. I realised I was in the presence of a saint. 'No', he said, 'my place is with my people, and now your place is with yours.'

In the audience was Fr Donald Monan SJ who had been president of Boston College when his Jesuit brothers at his sister university were assassinated. With other Jesuit university presidents from the United States, he went to El Salvador and sat through the trial of the soldiers indicted with the killings. He spent years lobbying United States congressmen to withdraw support for the unaccountable military in El Salvador, observing, 'The intellectual architects of this crime have never been publicly identified' or called to account.

When Ellacuria became rector of UCA he said that his country was 'an unjust and irrational reality that should be transformed' and that the university needed to contribute to social change: 'It does this in a university manner and with a Christian inspiration.' When

Monan returned from El Salvador, he was fond of telling his students: 'We must do all we can to ensure that freedom predominates over oppression, justice over injustice, truth over falsehood, and love over hatred. If the university does not decide to make this commitment, we do not understand what validity it has as a university, much less as a Christian inspired university.'

Learned Catholics all need to have an engagement in this honest and open debate, respecting the competencies of all, and inspired by Pope Francis's vision of St Francis of Assisi who is the model of the inseparable bond 'between concern for nature, justice for the poor, commitment to society, and interior peace'.[22] Hopefully we are now free to express the view that Francis's splendid encyclical would be all the stronger if it conceded that the growth in the world's human population—from 2 billion when Pius XII first spoke of contraception to 3.5 billion when Paul VI promulgated *Humanae Vitae* to 7.3 billion and climbing as it is today—points to a need to reconsider the Church's teaching on contraception. The pope is quite right to insist that the reduction of population growth is not the only solution to the environmental crisis. But it is part of the solution. It may even be an essential part of the solution. Banning contraception in a world of 7.3 billion people confronting the challenges of climate change and loss of biodiversity is a very different proposition from banning it in a world of only 2 billion people oblivious of such challenges. Think only of the ecological damage which would have occurred if all persons on the planet had been following the papal teaching on birth control since 1968. The human contribution to climate change and loss of biodiversity would hardly have been an improvement.

Celebrating the 50th anniversary of Vatican II and preparing for the forthcoming Synod on the Family, we can take heart from the changes in our Church which permit and encourage such questions and dialogue. One effect of the recent encyclical *Laudato Si'* is that it is no longer just liberal Catholics who are labelled as cafeteria Catholics. Some erstwhile conservative Catholics and papal apologists have become very exceptionalist in their discussion of this encyclical. We are now all welcome to the real world of questioning engagement in a Church that we cherish for its teaching office and sense of tradition.

---

22. Pope Francis, Address to Members of Communications Media, 16 March 2013, #11.

John O'Malley SJ, the finest contemporary historian of Vatican II writing in the English language has provided us with 'a simple litany' of the changes in church style indicated by the council's vocabulary: 'from commands to invitations, from laws to ideals, from threats to persuasion, from coercion to conscience, from monologue to conversation, from ruling to serving, from withdrawn to integrated, from vertical and top-down to horizontal, from exclusion to inclusion, from hostility to friendship, from static to changing, from passive acceptance to active engagement, from prescriptive to principled, from defiant to open-ended, from behaviour modification to conversion of heart, from the dictates of law to the dictates of conscience, from external conformity to the joyful pursuit of holiness.'[23]

Looking to the future, let's sustain each other in hope. Working from the strength of our tradition and from the immediacy of our contact with the marginalised, we can contribute to the culture, public dialogue, and legal structures necessary for enhancing human dignity and public order for all.

---

23. John W O'Malley, 'Vatican II: Did Anything Happen?', in *Vatican II: Did Anything Happen?*, edited by David G Scholthoven (London/New York" Continuum, 2007), 81.

Chapter 2

Autonomy and the Common Good

The case study of law and policy relating to euthanasia and physician-assisted suicide

---

On 3 February 2015, the United Kingdom House of Commons after a brief but spirited debate voted by 382 to 128 to approve the *Human Fertilization and Embryology (Mitochondrial Donation) Regulations*. The regulations clear the path for scientists to use maternal spindle transfer (MST) or pro-nuclear transfer (PNT) in attempts to rectify mitochondrial diseases caused by defects in the mitochondria of cells. MST occurs when the nucleus of a prospective mother's egg with a mitochondrial deficiency is removed and placed in the enucleated egg from another woman without any mitochondrial deficiency. The healthy egg can then be united with the prospective father's sperm hopefully producing a healthy child with no inherited mitochondrial deficiency. PNT occurs when the nucleus of an embryo with a mitochondrial deficiency is removed and placed in another enucleated embryo without any mitochondrial deficiency. In each case, scientists assure us that the resulting healthy baby carries the genetic inheritance only or almost exclusively of the mother and the father. Critics of the proposed procedure claim that the baby has three parents, including the outside party whose egg or embryo was enucleated to provide the resultant healthy egg or embryo.

The regulation approved by the Parliament allows the Human Fertilisation and Embryology Authority (HFEA), the United Kingdom's statutory regulator overseeing the use of gametes and embryos in fertility treatment and research, to license such procedures.

A week before the parliamentary debate a letter was published in *The Times* by leading scientists and ethicists including Baroness Warnock saying:

> The question that parliamentarians must consider is not whether they would want to use this technology themselves, but whether there are good grounds to prevent affected families from doing so. We believe that those who know what it is like to care for, and sometimes to lose, an extremely sick child are the people best placed to decide whether this technology is right for them, with medical advice and within the strict regulatory framework proposed. They have been waiting for the science for long enough. They should not have to wait for the law to catch up.[1]

Her co-signatories included people like Sir John Sulston and Sir Robert Nurse, biologist and geneticist respectively, both Nobel Peace Prize winners, and the Reverend Lord Harries, retired Anglican Bishop of Oxford.

Those parliamentarians opposed to granting the HFEA the power to authorise such procedures raised three types of concern. Some thought any such tinkering with human cells and/or reproduction was just plainly wrong. Some thought that it may be justified but that there was a need for greater clarity as to where such tinkering would stop—the slippery slope argument. If tinkering to correct deficiencies were permitted, why not permit tinkering to enhance human capacities, changing the DNA of the nucleus and not just of the mitochondria? Is this the door which once prized open for the most laudable of motives leads to the creation of the super-race of designer babies? Some thought there had been insufficient testing of the procedure in non-human primates and that such experimentation carried inordinate risks. It was just too early to allow adventurous medical researchers and anxious prospective parents to start experimenting in this way. Jim Shannon told Parliament:

> It must be remembered that the United States Food and Drug Administration considered the techniques last year and decided that there was not enough preclinical evidence

---

1. *The Times*, 28 January 2015.

to justify proceeding. I understand that the same body has reopened the debate and has insisted that it will be at least two years before it is ready to make a judgment.[2]

Sir Edward Leigh made the historical observation: "The FDA, of course, refused to allow the use of Thalidomide while we did, and the rest, as they say, is history."[3]

Regarding the slippery slope arguments, Jane Ellison, the Minister introducing the Regulation told Parliament: 'It is defined in primary legislation that the regulations can apply only to serious mitochondrial disease. There is no slippery slope. I looked back at the debates in the House on IVF all those years ago, when some were worried about a slippery slope, and all the safeguards are still in place more than two decades later.'[4]

In the lead up to the parliamentary debate, the two major Christian denominations in the United Kingdom, the Catholics and Anglicans, published positions by their relevant church leaders. The Anglicans were 'supportive, in principle, of both MST and PNT', but thought further research was necessary 'into the relationship between mtDNA and nDNA.'[5] The Catholic church leadership was more assertive. Their spokesman Bishop John Sherrington said, 'Many people are rightly concerned about the profound implications of Parliament passing regulations under the Human Fertilisation and Embryology Act to licence the creation of human embryos using the DNA of three people.'[6] He also expressed concerns about the need for prior clinical tests and objected to any procedure which would involve the destruction of embryos.

---

2. House of Commons, *Hansard*, 3 February 2015 : Column 182.
3. House of Commons, *Hansard*, 3 February 2015: Column 167.
4. House of Commons, *Hansard*, 3 February 2015: Column 186.
5. Church of England, *Mission and Public Affairs Council Submission to the Human Fertilisation and Embryology Authority Consultation*, December 2102 available at https://churchofengland.org/media-centre/news/2015/01/statement-from-revd-dr-brendan-mccarthy-on-mitochondrial-replacement-therapy.aspx.
6. Bishop John Sherrington, Department for Christian Responsibility and Citizenship, *Statement on Mitochondrial Donation*, 30 January 2015, available at http://www.catholic-ew.org.uk/Home/News/Mitochondrial-Donation.

During the parliamentary debate, opponents of the regulation invoked the churches and their concerns. The Minister Jane Ellison was able to inform the House:

> I have today spoken with the right reverend Prelate the Bishop of Carlisle, who speaks for the Church of England on ethical matters in the other place, and with the Rev Dr Brendan McCarthy, the Church's national adviser on medical ethics, and they have told me that I can confirm that the Church is not opposed in principle to mitochondrial donation.[7]

Splitting the churches, the government was able to negate further their impact on the debate. After the regulations were approved, a prominent Catholic moral theologian Fr Jack Mahoney SJ published his assessment, approving maternal spindle transfer (MST) which does not involve the destruction of any embryo but only of an unfertilized egg and expressing reservations about pro-nuclear transfer (PNT) which does necessitate the destruction of embryos. With a refreshing tone open to dialogue, he wrote:

> Those who hold to the moral position maintained by the Church of respecting the integrity of the human embryo from the time of its conception will have very serious reservations about using this less common method, whose success involves the destruction of a human embryo. It is therefore in the interests of respecting this view, as well as of finding the widest possible approval and support for the principle of genetic transplantation, to concentrate attention and practice on the earlier means mentioned, that of starting from two eggs, rather than creating two embryos and discarding one.
>
> It is considerations such as those that we have been examining here that could lead us to take a cool but sympathetic look at modern medical developments, including those affecting human reproduction, and to admire and welcome whenever possible the steps being offered to prevent personal and family tragedies.[8]

---

7. House of Commons, *Hansard*, 3 February 2015 : Column 186.
8. *The Tablet*, 7 February 2015.

In response, the Catholic Church hierarchy's official representative on the issue, Bishop John Sherrington broadened his previously stated objections to the regulation, lamenting its passing, and expressing objections to MST even if it could be developed safely and even though it did not involve the destruction of embryos. These were his three concerns:

> First, the gift of a new human life should arise from an act of love through sexual intercourse in which parents give themselves to each other in a fully human way and should not become the result of technological manipulation. Only in this way do we show due reverence to the mystery of life.
>
> Second, the impact of this procedure on the woman who donates the egg needs greater moral consideration. She is not just donating any tissue: her donation is inextricably linked with the creation of new life. In addition, the word 'donor' is used loosely; there is the real danger that this procedure further exploits women in the area of human reproduction.
>
> Third, we are increasingly aware of how personal and genetic identity is important to people. Is it not significant for the child to know the mother who donated the egg and recognise that she is in fact far more than a tissue donor? How will children's rights be protected in this regard?[9]

MST if safe and if successful will not affect the hereditary characteristics of the child. So the mother who donated the egg will not be a contributor to the child's hereditary characteristics. This is different from the situation of a gamete donor. I think there is little compelling in the argument that the child be entitled to know the identity of the one who donated the good mitochondria. Successful mitochondrial replacement will affect human germ lines, impacting on successive generations. So it is essential that its effects be fully understood. Of course any new procedure must be regulated in such a way as to avoid the exploitation of women. There is little point, even within closed Catholic church circles where IVF enjoys much the same level of support as in the community generally, to be putting the argument that respect for reverence for life can be expressed only through the creation of embryos by acts of sexual intercourse without

---

9. *The Tablet*, 21 February 2015.

the use of any assisted reproductive techniques. Many couples, including many Catholic couples, think they are showing the ultimate respect for human life by seeking to create a child through IVF in co-operation with doctors who do their best to avoid the creation of excess of embryos in the process.

As with many medical developments, it is always sensible to inquire where the new developments might lead. Those with ethical or prudential concerns about a new development might raise the slippery slope argument: if we follow course A1, might it not then lead to A2, A3, and ultimately A4, and whatever our disagreement about A1, none of us would embrace A4. Jack Mahoney invoked the *bon mot* which he attributed to Baroness Warnock (but which is usually said to be the progeny of John Harris): 'On slippery slopes, whether you can keep your footing or not depends on whether you are wearing skis or crampons'. Crampons are not familiar to those of us from down under. They are boots with spikes designed for rock and ice climbing. One of Mahoney's critics said the comparison of crampons and skis was facile when 'we are surrounded by legislators who openly proclaim they are on snowboards'.[10]

The passage of this United Kingdom regulation provides a good case study of the key issues I want to investigate under the title Autonomy and the Common Good. Countries like the United States, Canada, the United Kingdom and Australia have much in common; as already noted, they also have great differences, including different constitutional arrangements with contrasting checks and balances, and with starkly contrasting distributions of decision making power between elected politicians and unelected judges. They each have a robust civil society. They each have a public square which harbours a deep suspicion about those with religious viewpoints, convictions, and beliefs, while conceding that those with diverse comprehensive world views are entitled to a place at the table of public deliberation or at what the Oxford theologian Nigel Biggar calls 'the table of public negotiation'. Biggar says one cannot take a seat at that table unless one has 'a readiness to negotiate and so to persuade; and that has implications for what one does at the table, for how one behaves. To persuade, one must become persuasive'. It is in the respectful dialogue of those with differing perspectives that one hopes to reach the right

---

10. William Charlton, *The Tablet*, 21 February 2015.

or preferable answer about difficult policy questions, striking the right balance between autonomy and the common good. There is no point in appealing to religious authority; it would be counter-productive and discourteous to do so. Arguments must speak for themselves or at least be comprehensible and appealing to those who accord no status to religious authority. As Biggar says,

> [I]f I, a religious believer, am going to succeed in persuading you, an agnostic or atheist or different kind of religious believer, of my moral view, then I will have to show you that your view has weaknesses or problems, that these cannot be adequately repaired in your terms, but that they can be repaired in mine.[11]

The first step might be for the religious believer to convince the secularist interlocutor that better ethical outcomes for laws and policies can result if we follow due process and makes changes only after careful inquiry, affirming that we need to apply proper crampons while navigating and maintaining our stand on precarious slopes which may easily turn slippery.

The late American physician-ethicist Ed Pellegrino once pointed out:

> The slippery slope is not a myth. Historically it has been a reality in world affairs. Once a moral precept is breached a psychological and logical process is set in motion which follows what I would call the law of infinite regress of moral exceptions. One exception leads logically and psychologically to another. In small increments a moral norm eventually obliterates itself. The process always begins with some putative good reason, like compassion, freedom of choice, or liberty. By small increments it overwhelms its own justifications.[12]

It is questionable whether we have enough in our philosophical toolbox when dealing with difficult new social questions if the

---

11. Nigel Biggar, 'Why Religion Deserves a Place in Secular Medicine', in *Journal of Medical Ethics*, 41 (2015): 229 at 230.
12. Edward Pellegrino, 'Physician-Assisted Suicide and Euthanasia: Rebuttals of Rebuttals—The Moral Prohibition Remains', *Journal of Medicine and Philosophy*, 26/1 (2001): 93–100 at 98.

only instruments available are autonomy, human rights and non-discrimination. All those involved at the table of public negotiation (regardless of their comprehensive world views, whether religious or not) are entitled to express skepticism about the adequate testing of any new proposal and to seek answers to the likely next steps should the proposal be implemented. They are also entitled to agitate the question whether the proposal is ethically sound according to the diverse ethical views held in the community.

Let me now turn to physician-assisted suicide—one of the difficult slopes our legislators and judges will need to navigate in the coming years.

With medical advances, there has been a rapid increase in our life expectancy in our societies. Here in the United States life expectancy has increased from seventy years to seventy-nine years since 1960. Advances in technology allow us to maintain life for those suffering acute physical impairment, including those rendered quadriplegic by sporting and other accidents. Even without advances in technology, with better quality nursing care alone, we are able to maintain a long life for those suffering long term degenerative diseases. As people live longer, there is the increasing prospect that their bodies will outlive their minds. Human dignity and autonomy become vexed policy considerations when caring for persons with dementia often brought on by Alzheimer's disease.

In hindsight it is now clear that our societies left behind the stable terrain of a non-discriminatory universal approach to suicide when they first decriminalized attempted suicide. The criminal law was seen as having no useful role to play in stopping citizens from attempting suicide. In fact the blunt instrument of the criminal law could act as a disincentive for people to seek help with their suicidal ideation. The state through laws and policies could and still did espouse the sanctity of human life, setting up programs aimed at encouraging vulnerable persons not to consider suicide as an option. But the law has unwittingly set out on a slippery slope of discriminatory outcomes which were said not to extend autonomy and human dignity to all equally.

Once the offence of attempted suicide was abolished, the self-determining person without a disability was able to attempt to take their own life without any fear of state intervention. The question then arose: why should not the person with disability be able to invoke assistance so as to achieve the same outcome as the result of an autonomous choice, a self-determining decision, equally respected by the state? State officials conceded that there were instances when it would be compassionate, appropriate or at least a matter of supreme state indifference for a loved one to assist a person with a disability to commit suicide provided only that the deceased had made a free and informed decision and that the loved one had not acted out of any self-interest or for any motive other than seeking to help the deceased.

So then the question arose: should the offence of assisting with suicide be abolished, or at least should there be a legislated exemption for those genuinely acting on behalf of the deceased and acting in their best interests?

The next step on the slope whether one is wearing judicial or legislative crampons is the stretch of path where those without a disability, preferring assistance with suicide rather than having to do it alone, seek equal treatment with those suffering a disability. If a person with a disability is able to invoke assistance in dying, why shouldn't any other person also be able to invoke assistance if that is their self determining preference? What interest does the state have in ensuring that the person without a disability dies at their own hand rather than with assistance at their specific direction, provided only that the decision is made freely and conscientiously, with all appropriate safeguards against abuse? So how can the state justify any ban on assistance with suicide provided only that there are safeguards against involuntariness, coercion or incapacity to make a free, informed decision?

The next turn on the path leads to a fork in the road leading to a choice between the higher road and the one less travelled. The higher road is the maintained regimen for dissuading members of the community generally from pursuing suicide with assistance, while the road less travelled is the path made available only to those who are terminally ill, expecting to die in a short time (say six months) from an inevitably progressive condition which cannot be reversed by treatment, and with the proviso that they have to be able to self-administer the hemlock prepared for them by their willing helper. Over time, the question then becomes: why should this path be restricted only to that group? What about the long term stroke victim or the quadriplegic ex-footballer?

Having left behind the stable terrain of a non-discriminatory universal ban on suicide, we are sure to find that there is no stable terrain immune from challenge on the basis of autonomy, human rights and non-discrimination until we reach the valley where there is once again a non-discriminatory universal approach to suicide: all persons are entitled to state authorised assistance with suicide provided only that the state is able to confirm that the individual decision is free and informed. Coming down the path we will have thrown off those considerations of the common good or state interest such as those enunciated by the lower court in the *Washington* v *Glucksberg* litigation: '(1) preserving life; (2) preventing suicide; (3) avoiding the involvement of third parties and use of arbitrary, unfair, or undue influence; (4) protecting family members and loved ones; (5) protecting the integrity of the medical profession; and (6) avoiding future movement toward euthanasia and other abuses.'[13] Chief Justice Rehnquist delivering the opinion of the United States Supreme Court expanded on these state interests listing: 'an unqualified interest in the preservation of human life'; 'preserving the lives of those who can still contribute to society and have the potential to enjoy life'; 'preventing suicide, and studying, identifying and treating its causes'; protecting 'depressed or mentally ill persons, or those who are suffering from untreated pain, from suicidal impulses'; 'protecting the integrity and ethics of the medical profession'; maintaining 'the trust that is essential to the doctor-patient relationship' by avoiding the blurring of 'the time honored line between healing and harming'; 'protecting vulnerable groups—including the poor, the elderly, and disabled persons—from abuse, neglect and mistakes'; protecting disabled and terminally ill people from prejudice, negative and

---

13. Quoted by Chief Justice Rehnquist in footnote 20 in *Washington* v *Glucksberg* 521 U. S. 702, 728 (1997). In a further footnote, Chief Justice Rehnquist noted, 'Respondents also admit the existence of these interests, but contend that Washington could better promote and protect them through regulation, rather than prohibition, of physician-assisted suicide. Our inquiry, however, is limited to the question whether the State's prohibition is rationally related to legitimate state interests.' (see footnote 21 at p 728).

inaccurate stereotypes, and 'societal indifference'; avoiding 'the path to voluntary and perhaps even involuntary euthanasia'.[14]

This winding and slippery path I have postulated is not a figment of my imagination. Twenty two years ago, Justice Sopinka of the narrow majority in the Canadian Supreme Court decision (5-4) upheld the ban on assistance with suicide as 'there was no halfway measure that could be relied upon with assurance' to protect the vulnerable.[15] Justice McLachlin in dissent stated the assumption about the last plateau of stable terrain and asked the key question about how far one would then need to travel down the path whether with crampons or skis. She said, 'Assuming without deciding that Parliament could criminalise all suicides, whether assisted or not, does the fact that suicide is not criminal make the criminalisation of all assistance in suicide arbitrary?'[16] With greater specificity we might ask, does the fact that suicide is not criminal make the criminalisation of any assistance with an assuredly voluntary suicide arbitrary? In the case of the 42 year old Sue Rodriguez suffering Lou Gehrig's Disease (amyotrophic lateral sclerosis (ASL)), Justice McLachlin, unlike Chief Justice Rehnquist three years later, could countenance only one conceivable state interest to justify denying Ms Rodriguez 'the capacity to treat her body in a way available to the physically able': the prospect that it might 'open the doors, if not the floodgates, to the killing of disabled persons who may not truly consent to death'. Convinced that this state interest could be accommodated with strict safeguards to ensure free and informed consent, she said Ms Rodriquez was being asked to serve 'as a scapegoat' and that the most that would be needed would be 'a further stipulation requiring court orders to permit the assistance of suicide in a particular case'.[17]

Does the state have an interest in having its citizens generally encouraged not to commit suicide, acknowledging that state authorised medical assistance does decrease the personal resistance to going through with a commitment to suicide? Is the state interest less or different when it comes to those who are terminally ill and facing the immediate prospect of death? If so, what about those who

---

14. *Washington* v *Glucksberg* 521 U. S. 702, 728-32 (1997).
15. *Rodriguez* v *BC (AG)* [1993] 3 SCR 519, 614.
16. *Rodriguez* v *BC (AG)* [1993] 3 SCR 519 , 620.
17. *Rodriguez* v *BC (AG)* [1993] 3 SCR 519, 627.

are permanently incapacitated or suffering a long term condition which inevitably leads to death but only after a significant period of time? Is there a state interest in withholding state approval for assistance with their death on the basis that the state has an interest in providing a culture and a structure which is supportive of people choosing life rather than death, as distinguished from those choosing how and when to die, given that they will die imminently, and that they are simply wanting to hasten death or structure their dying in a more dignified or manageable way? These are the sorts of questions which need to be answered at the table of public deliberation and negotiation. They are questions which occasion discomfort not only to those who espouse a religious view or comprehensive world view which includes an acknowledgement of the sacredness and the giftedness of human life, but also to those who see no need for law or policy to seek to protect or enhance any interests or outcomes other than the autonomous decisions of individuals empowered to determine the moment and manner of their death.

In February 2015, the Canadian Supreme Court under the Chief Justiceship of Justice McLachlin unanimously ruled that the absolute ban on assisting someone to commit suicide was unconstitutional.[18] Those south of the border need to understand that this court under the leadership of Chief Justice McLachlin has real constitutional wind in its sails. In January the court discovered a free standing constitutional right to strike in their *Charter of Rights and Freedoms* with Justice Abela saying it was 'time to give this conclusion constitutional benediction' and that 'clearly the arc bends increasingly towards workplace justice.'[19] In their journey towards constitutional recognition of the right to strike, the majority even took heart from the fact that countries like France and Portugal had included the right to strike in their Constitutions prior to the enactment of the Canadian Charter. The two dissenters had the temerity to observe, 'If anything the absence of an express right to strike in the Charter—which was enacted subsequent to many of the Constitutions cited by the majority—indicates Parliament and the provincial legislatures' intention to exclude such a right.'[20]

---

18. *Carter* v *Canada (Attorney General)*, 2015 SCC 5.
19. *Saskatchewan Federation of Labor* v *Saskatchewan*, 2015 SCC 4, [1], [4].
20. *Saskatchewan Federation of Labor* v *Saskatchewan*, 2015 SCC 4, [158].

The activist Canadian Court has now reversed its previous decision upholding the ban on assisted suicide twenty-one years ago, noting there have been changes to the law and end of life care in other places, as well as to the Court's way of interpreting the Canadian *Charter of Rights and Freedoms*. The court has suspended its judgment for a year giving the Parliament time to consider how it will respond.

The court considered the claims of two parties. In 2009, Gloria Taylor was diagnosed with Lou Gehrig's Disease (ALS), the same condition as was suffered by Sue Rodriquez. Gloria Taylor knew that she would first lose the ability to use her hands and feet, and that she would progressively lose the capacity to chew, swallow, speak and breathe. She did 'not want to die slowly, piece by piece' or 'wracked with pain'. She wanted to have the option of seeking medical assistance to self-administer a painless, deadly potion at a time of her choosing. She explained:

> There will come a point when I will know that enough is enough. I cannot say precisely when that time will be. It is not a question of 'when I can't walk' or 'when I can't talk'. There is no preset trigger moment. I just know that, globally, there will be some point in time when I will be able to say—'this is it, this is the point where life is just not worthwhile'. When that time comes, I want to be able to call my family together, tell them of my decision, say a dignified goodbye and obtain final closure—for me and for them.[21]

Having commenced the long running litigation, Gloria Taylor passed away in 2012 from natural causes.

In 2008 Kay Carter had been diagnosed with spinal stenosis, a condition that results in the progressive compression of the spinal cord. She told her family that she did not want to end her life 'like an ironing board', having to lie flat in bed all day and all night. In 2010, she convinced her daughter Lee and Lee's husband Hollis to accompany her to Switzerland so she could obtain assistance with dying from *Dignitas*. Lee and Hollis joined the litigation seeking court assurance that they could not be prosecuted for having assisted Kay with her suicide.

---

21. *Carter v Canada (Attorney General)*, 2015 SCC 5, [12].

The *Canadian Charter of Rights and Freedoms* provides in section 7: 'Everyone has the right to life, liberty and security of the person and the right not to be deprived thereof except in accordance with the principles of fundamental justice'. The successful argument put by those seeking approval for assisted suicide ran as follows.

Gloria or Kay is entitled to take her own life at a time of her choosing. If she is denied the capacity to seek assistance with her suicide, she will need to end her life sooner than she otherwise would have chosen because she will need to do it when she is still physically able to arrange her death. If she were permitted to seek assistance she could live longer. The criminal sanction banning assistance with suicide thereby deprives her of some span of life because she needs to choose a premature death.

The Supreme Court agreed with the trial judge who decided that 'the right to life is engaged where the law or state action imposes death or an increased risk of death on a person, either directly or indirectly', regardless of whether death is being chosen by the person claiming the right to life.'[22] Considering the right to liberty and security of the person in the context of the personal decision when to commit suicide, the court observed, 'This is a decision that is rooted in their control over their bodily integrity; it represents their deeply personal response to serious pain and suffering. By denying them the opportunity to make that choice, the prohibition impinges on their liberty and security of the person.'[23] So the court ruled that insofar as the criminal law prohibited 'physician-assisted dying for competent adults who seek such assistance as a result of a grievous and irremediable medical condition that causes enduring and intolerable suffering', it 'infringes the rights to liberty and security of the person'.[24]

Under the Canadian Charter, once a *prima facie* infringement of a section 7 right is found, it is then necessary to determine whether that infringement is in accordance with 'the principles of fundamental justice'. The court looks to whether the impingement on life, liberty or security is arbitrary, overbroad or has consequences that are grossly disproportionate to the law's object. The Court decided that the only

---

22. *Carter v Canada (Attorney General)*, 2015 SCC 5, [62].
23. *Carter v Canada (Attorney General)*, 2015 SCC 5, [68].
24. *Carter v Canada (Attorney General)*, 2015 SCC 5, [68]..

object of the prohibition on assisted suicide was the state's need and desire to protect vulnerable persons from being induced to commit suicide at a time of weakness. It would not countenance the generic preservation of life as a legitimate object. Neither did the court consider objects such as the desire to enhance the value of life for all persons and to dissuade community members from considering such an option to life's problems, both because of the prospective loss to the community of the person who suicides and the devastating and demoralising effects suicide can have on others. The court took it upon itself to reject any broad object for the prohibition because it then 'becomes difficult to say that the means used to further it are overbroad or disproportionate'.[25] One might equally say that to narrow the object as the court did makes it impossible to decide other than that the law is overbroad or disproportionate. Contrary to the submissions put by Canada, the court decided that 'the direct target of the measure (enacted by the Canadian Parliament) is the narrow goal of preventing vulnerable persons from being induced to commitsuicide at a time of weakness'.[26] Why could the court not postulate a broader object for the prohibition on the provision of assistance with suicide, namely dissuading or discouraging (without preventing or prohibiting) all persons from being induced to commit suicide? Having narrowed the object of the law, the court had no problem in determining that the prohibition on assisted suicide was overbroad

At the trial, the state conceded 'that not every person who wishes to commit suicide is vulnerable, and that there may be people with disabilities who have a considered, rational and persistent wish to end their own lives'.[27] The trial judge observed that Gloria Taylor was one such person: 'competent, fully-informed, and free from coercion or duress'. On appeal the Supreme Court decided, 'The blanket prohibition sweeps conduct into its ambit that is unrelated to the law's objective'.[28]

Having decided that the absolute ban on assisted suicide was a breach of a Charter right, the court needed to consider whether the

---

25. *Carter* v *Canada (Attorney General)*, 2015 SCC 5, [77].
26. *Carter* v *Canada (Attorney General)*, 2015 SCC 5, [78].
27. *Carter* v *Canada (Attorney General)*, 2015 SCC 5, [86].
28. *Carter* v *Canada (Attorney General)*, 2015 SCC 5, [86]

breach was one which could be 'demonstrably justified in a free and democratic society'. In passing, I note the gratuitous observation of one of our more conservative Australian jurists with an Oxford bent who asked, 'What is the difference between that which is 'justified' and that which is 'demonstrably justified'? The shrill, intensifying adverb merely highlights the vacuity of the verb.'[29]

The Canadian court confirmed that it is 'difficult to justify a s.7 violation' and that the right to life, liberty and security was 'not easily overridden by competing social interests'[30]. The court usually grants Parliament some deference in making this assessment. But in this case the court observed that the blanket ban on assisted suicide could hardly be viewed as a 'complex regulatory response' to a social ill which would usually garner a high degree of deference.

The court needed to consider whether the absolute ban was the least drastic means of achieving the narrow legislative objective of protecting the vulnerable. The Supreme Court was adamant that a less drastic means was available. The court accepted the trial judge's conclusion that 'it is possible for physicians, with due care and attention to the seriousness of the decision involved, to adequately assess decisional capacity' and that 'the risks associated with physician-assisted death can be limited through a carefully designed and monitored system of safeguards.'[31]

It is disheartening to note the court's unquestioning acceptance of the trial judge's observation that the 'preponderance of the evidence from ethicists is that there is no ethical distinction between physician-assisted death and other end-of-life practices whose outcome is highly likely to be death.'[32] Those other practices are the withholding or withdrawal of lifesaving or life-sustaining medical treatment. The time honoured distinctions between act and omission and between intention and causation have been erased by judicial *fiat* and the straw vote of ethicists chosen by the parties to a legal dispute. There is now said to be no ethical distinction between turning off the ventilator and administering a lethal injection. The court has moved the debate very rapidly into choppy waters. The Canadian court saw no need to

---

29. Justice Dyson Heydon in *Momcilovic* v *The Queen* [2011] HCA 34, [428].
30. *Carter* v *Canada (Attorney General)*, 2015 SCC 5 [95].
31. *Carter* v *Canada (Attorney General)*, 2015 SCC 5, [117].
32. Quoted with approval in *Carter* v *Canada (Attorney General)*, 2015 SCC 5, [23].

refer to the robust and coherent view of the United States Supreme Court in *Vacco v Quill* when Chief Justice Rehnquist writing for the Court said:

> [W]e think the distinction between assisting suicide and withdrawing life-sustaining treatment, a distinction widely recognised and endorsed in the medical profession and in our legal traditions, is both important and logical; it is certainly rational. See *Feeney, supra*, at 272 ('When the basic classification is rationally based, uneven effects upon particular groups within a class are ordinarily of no constitutional concern').
>
> The distinction comports with fundamental legal principles of causation and intent. First, when a patient refuses life sustaining medical treatment, he dies from an underlying fatal disease or pathology; but if a patient ingests lethal medication prescribed by a physician, he is killed by that medication ...
>
> Furthermore, a physician who withdraws, or honors a patient's refusal to begin, life-sustaining medical treatment purposefully intends, or may so intend, only to respect his patient's wishes and 'to cease doing useless and futile or degrading things to the patient when [the patient] no longer stands to benefit from them.'[33]

It is staggering to see the Court's dismissal of concerns about possible abuses that have occurred in other jurisdictions. The court showed deference to the trial judge's findings that 'there was no evidence of inordinate impact on socially vulnerable populations in the permissive jurisdictions'.[34] Following the trial judge's assessment and quoting her finding, the Supreme Court said, 'Expert evidence established that the 'predicted abuse and disproportionate impact on vulnerable populations has not materialised' in Belgium, the Netherlands and Oregon.'[35] The Supreme Court received expert evidence about abuses in Belgium, with the expert concluding that 'once euthanasia is allowed, it becomes very difficult to maintain a strict interpretation of the statutory conditions.'[36] The expert evidence of abuse failed to

---

33. *Vacco v Quill*, 521 U. S. 793, 800–1 (1997).
34. *Carter v Canada (Attorney General)*, 2015 SCC 5, [107].
35. *Carter v Canada (Attorney General)*, 2015 SCC 5, [25].
36. *Carter v Canada (Attorney General)*, 2015 SCC 5, [111].

convince the court to review its deference to the trial judge's findings. Even if there were abuses as attested by the expert evidence, the court agreed with the trial judge that 'the permissive regime in Belgium is the product of a very different medico-legal culture'[37] and the Belgian cases 'offer little insight into how a Canadian regime might operate'.[38] The 2012 Belgian case of the deaf identical twins Marc and Eddy Verbessem who were granted euthanasia on learning that they would eventually go blind from what was said to be an untreatable glaucoma demonstrates just how permissive any regime can become. Marc and Eddy who lived together were still working up until the time of their death. They were not suffering any terminal illness. They were not in any physical pain. As far as the Canadian Supreme Court was concerned, there may be evidence of such abuses in Belgium, but even if there were, that is immaterial to any consideration in Canada because Canada is so different that no such abuses could be considered possible.

One might contrast this approach with that of Justice Souter on the United States Supreme Court when he noted the contested evidence about abuse in the Netherlands, with some commentators marshaling evidence 'that the Dutch guidelines have in practice failed to protect patients from involuntary euthanasia and have been violated with impunity'.[39] Deciding to stay his judicial hand and leave the matter to the legislature which has 'superior opportunities to obtain the facts necessary for a judgment about the present controversy', he said, 'The day may come when we can say with some assurance which side is right, but for now it is the substantiality of the factual disagreement, and the alternatives for resolving it, that matter. They are, for me, dispositive of the due process claim at this time.'[40]

The issue is now in the hands of Parliament. If the Canadian Parliament were just to sit on its hands, there would be no ban or regulation whatever of assisted suicide in place in a year's time. Presumably the Parliament will see a need to legislate a complex regulatory response, including the ongoing criminalisation of assistance with suicide other than that considered by the court.

---

37. *Carter* v *Canada (Attorney General)*, 2015 SCC 5, [112].
38. *Carter* v *Canada (Attorney General)*, 2015 SCC 5, [113].
39. *Washington* v *Glucksberg*, 521 US 702, 786 (1997).
40. *Washington* v *Glucksberg*, 521 US 702, 788, 786 (1997).

The court confined its attention to the case of 'physician-assisted death for a competent adult person who (1) clearly consents to the termination of life; and (2) has a grievous and irremediable medical condition (including an illness, disease or disability) that causes enduring suffering that is intolerable to the individual in the circumstances of his or her condition'. The court stated, 'We make no pronouncement on other situations where physician-assisted dying may be sought.'[41] Who then should decide competence, who should assess how grievous and irremediable a medical condition is, and who should decide whether the suffering is intolerable to the individual, especially if the individual be suffering some form of dementia? What safeguards need to be put in place? The court was satisfied 'that the risks associated with physician-assisted death can be limited through a carefully designed and monitored system of safeguards'.[42]

Nothing can be surer that once the Canadian Parliament has legislated a complex regulatory response for state authorised assisted suicide for the terminally ill or for those suffering diseases like Lou Gehrig's Disease, there will be applications to the court claiming that the regulatory response is discriminatory, working an arbitrary interference with the autonomy of other persons who seek the consolation of state authorised assistance with their voluntary suicide. The Canadian court has stepped across the line which the US Supreme Court wisely declined to cross in 1997, deferring to the state legislatures, when Chief Justice Rehnquist writing for the Court said:

> By extending constitutional protection to an asserted right or liberty interest, we, to a great extent, place the matter outside the arena of public debate and legislative action. We must therefore 'exercise the utmost care whenever we are asked to break new ground in this field,' lest the liberty protected by the Due Process Clause be subtly transformed into the policy preferences of the Members of this Court.[43]

There can be no doubt about the policy preferences of the members of the Supreme Court of Canada when it comes to physician-assisted suicide.

---

41. *Carter v Canada (Attorney General)*, 2015 SCC 5, [127].
42. *Carter v Canada (Attorney General)*, 2015 SCC 5 , [117].
43. *Washington v Glucksberg*, 521 US 702, 720 (1997).

The issue of assisted suicide has come regularly before the *European Court of Human Rights* in recent years. The *European Convention on Human Rights* recognises the unqualified right to life (Article 2) and respect for private life. Article 8 prohibits state interference with one's private life unless such interference 'is necessary in a democratic society . . . for the prevention of disorder or crime, for the protection of health or morals, or for the protection of the rights and freedoms of others'. In thirty-six of the forty-three member states, all assistance with suicide is prohibited and criminalised by law. In Germany, Estonia and Sweden, assistance is not a criminal offence. In Switzerland, Belgium, the Netherlands, and Luxembourg, medical practitioners can prescribe and administer lethal drugs subject to specific safeguards. Not surprisingly the Strasbourg Court has accorded a fairly wide margin of appreciation to states in relation to assisted suicide.

In the United Kingdom, there have been several failed attempts to legislate for assisted suicide. In recent years there has been only one successful prosecution of a person for assisting suicide. The accused was 'someone who provided petrol and a lighter to a vulnerable man known to have suicidal intent, and who subsequently suffered severe burns as a result'.[44] Meanwhile between 1998 and 2011, 215 people from the United Kingdom used the services of *Dignitas* in Switzerland. No one who provided assistance was prosecuted.[45]

Lord Joffe has four times introduced bills to the House of Lords seeking some form of legalised assistance with dying. Each bill has failed. Each time he confined his attention to physician-assisted suicide only for the terminally ill, thereby excluding those like the appellants in the Canadian Supreme Court. He told the House of Lords, 'I would not support further extension into the field of euthanasia, or support assisted dying for patients who are not terminally ill.'[46] He has passed the baton to Lord Falconer who is now making his second attempt with his *Assisted Dying Bill*. In 2010, Lord Falconer set up a commission on assisted dying. Falconer and the major funders of the

---

44. *R (on the application of Nicklinson and another)* v *Ministry of Justice*, [2014] UKSC 38, [48].
45. *R (on the application of Nicklinson and another)* v *Ministry of Justice*, [2014] UKSC 38, [48].
46. House of Lords, *Hansard*, 12 May 2006, col 1188.

commission favoured some liberalising of the law on assisted suicide. Wearing their crampons, and wanting to take only incremental steps, the commissioners could agree only to extending legally assured assistance with suicide to the mentally competent person with a terminal illness giving free and informed consent. Having heard from many people with disabilities, the commission decided not to recommend 'that a non-terminally ill person with significant physical impairments should be made eligible under any future legislation to request assistance in ending his or her life'.[47] They thought this was necessary so as 'to send a clear message that disabled people's lives are valued equally'. That would be considered a completely unacceptable, overbroad, discriminatory, legislative objective by the Canadian Supreme Court. The Commission thought that 'terminal illness' should be defined as 'an advanced, progressive, incurable condition that is likely to lead to the patient's death within the next 12 months'.[48] Though the commission heard from witnesses who would like the ability to specify in a legal document that they desired assistance with suicide should they later be suffering dementia, the Commission considered that 'the natural requirement of mental capacity is an essential safeguard for assisted dying legislation'.[49] They ruled out all state authorised assistance for non-competent persons. The Commission was opposed to the involvement of any tribunal or legal body deciding whether consent was free and informed. They thought this role could be best performed by health and social care professionals.

Lords Joffe and Falconer have contributed to a very long running debate in the House of Lords on Lord Falconer's *Assisted Dying Bill*. The bill restricts the assistance by a medical practitioner to preparing medicine for self-administration or preparing a device like one of Dr Philip Nitschke's machines for self-administration of the medicine. The bill specifies that 'the decision to self-administer the medicine and the final act of doing so must be taken by the person for whom the medicine has been prescribed'.[50]

---

47. The Commission on Assisted Dying, Report, Demos, 2011, 27.
48. The Commission on Assisted Dying, Report, Demos, 2011, 27.
49. The Commission on Assisted Dying, Report, Demos, 2011, 27.
50. clause 4(4), *Assisted Dying Bill 2014*.

In July 2014, Lord Falconer told the House of Lords, 'I have built on the Oregon model, but with more safeguards. I reject the Belgian and Dutch approach.'[51] He is anxious to avoid arguments about slippery slopes and developments in Belgium and the Netherlands where doctors have performed euthanasia on non-competent patients and on patients who are not suffering terminal illness. To get his bill through, Lord Falconer has been prepared to consider further safeguards. Looking to the United Kingdom Supreme Court's June 2014 decision in *R (on the application of Nicklinson) v Ministry of Justice*, he has favourably quoted the Chief Justice Lord Neuberger who wrote:

> A system whereby a judge or other independent assessor is satisfied in advance that someone has a voluntary, clear, settled, and informed wish to die and for his suicide then to be organised in an open and professional way, would, at least in my current view, provide greater and more satisfactory protection for the weak and vulnerable, than a system which involves a lawyer from the DPP's office inquiring, after the event, whether the person who had killed himself had such a wish, and also to investigate the actions and motives of any assister, who would, by definition, be emotionally involved and scarcely able to take, or even to have taken, an objective view.[52]

In July 2014, Lord Falconer told the Lords: 'Some say that the courts should be involved as an additional safeguard before an assisted death occurs. We should constructively consider that issue in Committee.'[53] His *Assisted Dying Bill* initially proposed that these issues be resolved just by the patient and their physician. Lord Pannick QC who had appeared for *Dignity and Choice in Dying* in the recent Supreme Court case, proposed amendments which won unanimous support in the Lords in November 2014. The Bill now proposes that a court order always be obtained confirming the court's satisfaction that the adult patient has 'a voluntary, clear, settled and informed wish

---

51. House of Lords, Hansard, 18 July 2014 : Column 776.
52. *R (on the application of Nicklinson and another)* v *Ministry of Justice*, [2014] UKSC 38, [108].
53. House of Lords, *Hansard*, 18 July 2014 : Column 777.

to end his or her own life' and the capacity to make the decision.[54] Two doctors would need to certify that the patient is terminally ill (being reasonably expected to die within six months) having made the decision voluntarily and on an informed basis without coercion or duress. Terminal illness is defined in the Bill as 'an inevitably progressive condition which cannot be reversed by treatment'[55].

Though the media perception in the United Kingdom is that Lord Falconer's bill as amended could provide a resolution of the issue, the tragic irony is that his bill does nothing to address the situation of those like the three appellants who brought the case in the United Kingdom Supreme Court. None of them was terminally ill; none of them was expected to die within six months. The late Tony Nicklinson had suffered a catastrophic stroke which left him completely paralysed. He lived for another seven years describing his life as 'dull, miserable, demeaning, undignified and intolerable'.[56] Paul Lamb had been completely immobile, able to move only his right hand, requiring twenty-four hour nursing care since his car accident twenty-four years previously. The third appellant known only as Martin had suffered a brainstem stroke six years previously. These are the sorts of tragic cases which will now need to be considered by courts and parliaments concerned to protect the vulnerable while providing for them and those others like Gloria Taylor and Kay Carter in the recent Canadian case. While still wearing their crampons as they descended the slope, the Canadian judges restricted their constitutional finding of a right to assistance with suicide to those with 'a grievous and irremediable medical condition (including an illness, disease or disability) that causes enduring suffering that is intolerable to the individual in the circumstances of his or her condition'. Presumably that will cover the cases of Tony Nicklinson, Paul Lamb and Martin. Indicating that their skis were nearby in the judicial closet, the Canadians did then say, 'We make no pronouncement on other situations where physician-assisted dying may be sought.'

No doubt the United States Supreme Court will be called upon to reconsider the issue which was last before that court in 1997. Last

---

54. clause 1(2)(a), *Assisted Dying Bill* 2014.
55. clause 2 (1) *Assisted Dying Bill* 2014.
56. Quoted in *R (on the application of Nicklinson and another)* v *Ministry of Justice*, [2014] UKSC 38, [3].

time around, the United States Court addressed the issue four years after the Canadian Supreme Court had done so. I doubt that the time lag will be as long this time. Last time the United States Court stayed its hand with the observation, 'Throughout the Nation, Americans are engaged in an earnest and profound debate about the morality, legality, and practicality of physician-assisted suicide. Our holding permits this debate to continue, as it should in a democratic society.'[57] All members of the United States court back then were content that the States were 'undertaking extensive and serious evaluation of physician-assisted suicide and other related issues'. Justice O'Connor spoke of the 'challenging task of crafting appropriate procedures for safeguarding . . . liberty interests (being) entrusted to the "laboratory" of the States . . . in the first instance.'[58] Instead of talking about 'principles of fundamental justice' and what can be 'demonstrably justified in a free and democratic society', the United States judges will discuss 'due process' and 'equal protection'. These are the various constitutional devices for determining the judicial morality of vexed social questions. Societies like Canada, the United Kingdom and the United States are now at the frontier determining whether the administration of a fatal injection is the same as switching off a ventilator and whether state assisted and state authorised suicide should be restricted only to some groups or made available to all self-determining citizens whether or not they are suffering a painful terminal illness. In striking the necessary balance between individual autonomy and the common good, Lord Sumption put it well in the United Kingdom Supreme Court:

> There is no complete solution to the problem of protecting vulnerable people against an over-ready resort to suicide . . . The real question about all of these possibilities is how much risk to the vulnerable are we prepared to accept in this area in order to facilitate suicide for the invulnerable . . . There is an important element of social policy and moral value-judgment involved. The relative importance of the right to commit suicide and the right of the vulnerable to be protected from overt or covert pressure to kill themselves is inevitably

---

57. *Washington v Glucksberg*, 521 US 702, 720 (1997).
58. *Washington v Glucksberg*, 521 US 702, 737 (1997).

sensitive to a state's most fundamental collective moral and social values.[59]

The Canadian Supreme Court has decided that this sort of balancing exercise is no longer constitutionally possible. And yet it is essential in any society which prides itself on the protection of the vulnerable. Seeking to determine the limits on any right to physician-assisted suicide while answering the interlocutor who says, 'My life is my property, and I have the right to dispose of it when and how I choose', Biggar replies:

> 'Whether or not you have such a right is not something that you can establish merely by asserting it. It depends on whether or not you are subject to overriding obligations to other people, which constrain your choice of PAS or euthanasia'. Are there in fact such obligations? There would be, if granting a certain class of patient the right to PAS or euthanasia would undermine any societal commitment to support human life in adversity, and if it would expose a much larger number of patients to abusive manipulation. If that were the case, then larger considerations of social good would preclude the granting of a small class of individuals the right to PAS or euthanasia.[60]

The distinguished philosopher Baroness O'Neill when speaking against Lord Falconer's *Assisted Dying Bill* in the House of Lords observed how little the bill would actually assist people who do need help when they are dying, even though it would give a small group the right to assistance with suicide:[61]

> [T]he Bill does rather little to assist the dying. That noble purpose would require legislation that entitles all of us in our dying months, weeks and days to the necessary help and care, and pain relief, whether or not we are competent to choose. A Bill with those aims would have to address very large issues, above all the currently patchy availability of high-quality

---

59. *R (on the application of Nicklinson and another)* v *Ministry of Justice*, [2014] UKSC 38, [229].
60. Nigel Biggar, 'Why Religion Deserves A Place In Secular Medicine', in *Journal of Medical Ethics*, 41 (2015); 22, 232.
61. House of Lords, *Hansard*, 18 July 2014, Columns 781-2.

palliative care and incomplete availability of high-quality pain relief. This Bill proposes little to assist most of those who are dying. . . . This is not a Bill about assisting the dying.

[T]he Bill does little to support the choices of those who are dying. A Bill that centred on protecting the choice of those who are dying would concentrate on choices to refuse treatment, which can be, but so often are not, set out in advance directives, or choices about where to die. Do those who purport to care about the choices of the dying really have nothing to say about respecting or protecting the wholly uncontroversial choices of many who die on general wards, when they would have preferred to stay at home or in their nursing home with appropriate care and pain relief? Do they have nothing to say about choices that can be set out in advance directives? Seemingly so. The Bill supports only the choices of the few who might choose to commit suicide.

[T]he Bill is not about altering the law on suicide. . . .

[W]e are dealing with a proposal to amend the law on aiding and abetting suicide. There are many good reasons, which I need hardly spell out, why we need legislation that makes it an offence to aid and abet another's suicide. The question actually raised by the Bill is whether it is feasible or advisable to create an exemption for certain cases. The 1961 Act already provided that prosecution should not be automatic. In the wake of the *Coroners and Justice Act*, the Director of Public Prosecutions published a policy which sets out considerations for and against prosecution; and prosecutions are very few. However, this policy would be dislodged if the potential offence that warrants investigation or requires an inquest were abolished. The policy works because there is no immunity from investigation, from an inquest, or, if the facts of the case prove adverse, from prosecution. If there were no offence, none of these protections would remain. We shall have to see what case can be made for such a risky move.

Some of the Bill's proponents have recently publicly recommended it as a modest proposal. I wonder whether they have recently read Swift's great satirical essay that gave this notable phrase such long-lasting currency in our language.

You will recall that Jonathan Swift's 1729 satire *A Modest Proposal* was subtitled 'for preventing the children of poor people in Ireland from being a burden to their parents or country, and for making them beneficial to the public'. The proposal was quite simply that the poor Irish should eat their own children.

On June 27 2015, the American Foundation for Suicide Prevention hosted a 'Walk All Night to Fight Suicide'. Walkers were assured 'As you walk through the night, you'll feel safe and cared-for in a community where everyone supports each other. It's a place to laugh, to cry, and to heal—to honor the past and embrace a future that your work will change for the better.' Suicide is the fourth leading cause of death for adults between the ages of fifteen and sixty-four years in the United States (41,149 deaths in 2013). Ninety per cent of those who suicide have a diagnosable psychiatric disorder at the time of their death.[62] There is a legitimate state interest in seeking to arrest this alarming suicide rate. It is difficult to see how the extension of state authorised, often state funded, physician-assisted suicide to an expanding class of autonomous persons can be justified without some attempt to offset the inevitable consequences that increased state endorsement of suicide would effect. Some form of physician-assisted dying for those who are terminally ill is now permitted in Oregon, Washington, Vermont, New Mexico and arguably in Montana. Bills have been introduced into another fifteen state legislatures as well as the District of Columbia. The Montana lower house has now voted fifty-one to forty-eight prohibiting doctors from prescribing life-ending medication. In response, *The New York Times* editorial entitled 'Offering a Choice to the Terminally Ill' stated, 'As local lawmakers around the country debate the bills, they should consider how successfully and responsibly the law has been carried out in Oregon' where 105 terminally persons took their own lives last year by ingesting a medically prescribed lethal potion.[63]

Daniel Callahan from the Hastings Center has spoken of the organised obfuscation of the advocates for physician-assisted suicide. Having abandoned euthanasia after an abortive campaign in California in 1988, they now avoid the term 'suicide', with one newspaper reporter calling it 'a killer at the ballot box'. Using phrases like 'medically assisted death', 'hastened death', and 'patient-directed aid in dying', Callahan thinks the advocates disguise their real activity

---

62. See http://theovernight.donordrive.com/index.cfm?fuseaction=donorDrive.event&eventID=514.
63. *New York Times*, editorial, 15 March 2015.

and purpose which is the 'medicalisation of autonomy' and the 'medical legitimation' of suicide.[64]

You don't necessarily have to be Catholic or religious to think that doctors should do no harm, that patients are free to forego futile or burdensome treatment, and that palliative care be utilised to relieve pain. Suicide will occur from time to time, but why the need to enact laws conferring medical legitimation and increasing its likelihood? I readily concede that in Oregon, to date, they have maintained a bright line between euthanasia and physician-assisted suicide—but it's a line which has been dimmed by the Canadian Supreme Court's bright spotlight of autonomy. It is a line which would be extinguished were the Canadian judicial thinking to take hold south of the border. I do worry about the slippery slope for vulnerable patients who might think they have no option but taking their own lives. I remain committed to the simple Hippocratic Oath, 'Do no harm.' Do not take life. Care for the dying by relieving their suffering. And that is not just because I am Catholic.

As we wrestle with these issues, maintaining the balance between autonomy and the common good, let's keep our crampons on and 'maintain a convinced and pondered trust in the heritage of virtues and values handed down by our forebears'. Those of us with religiously informed ideas about the common good and human dignity need to be active participants in the intellectual and cultural dialogue which is 'essential to the discovery of truth in a historically conscious world'.[65] Any church interventions should, as David Hollenbach says, be 'carefully cast as documents that (seek) to persuade rather than coerce'.[66]

It will be some time before we come back to level ground. While welcoming a prosecutorial policy which does not threaten the compassion for, or the dignity of, those who assist invulnerable and competent, horrifically disabled persons like Sue Rodriguez, Gloria Taylor, Kay Carter Tony Nicklinson, Paul Lamb and Martin, let's continue to have a community care and a state concern for those

---

64. Daniel Callahan, 'Organized Obfuscation: Advocacy for Physician-Assisted Suicide', in *Hastings Center Report*, 38/5 (September-October 2008): 30, 32.
65. David Hollenbach, *The Global Face of Public Faith* (Georgetown: Georgetown University Press, 2003), 142.
66. Hollenbach, *The Global Face of Public Faith*, 144.

many others who can be dissuaded from suicide with society's legitimate concern and commitment to kill the pain and relieve the existential angst without killing the person, and leaving others to carry the burden of yet more suicides. The law needs to have a care for the dignity of all these persons, equally. Facilitating assistance with suicide for any autonomous person who wants it is not the way to enhance the dignity of those radically questioning the utility or worth of life that 'you'll feel safe and cared-for in a community where everyone supports each other'. We need to maintain the crampons on the slippery slope no matter what the superficial appeal of the judicial reasoning that we can extend autonomy, non-discrimination and individual human rights universally, all the way down to the valley of death.

'Three Biological Parent Babies' And Legalised 'Physician-Assisted Death':

What are their commonalities and where do we go from here?

Margaret Somerville

The short answer to the question in my title, 'Where do we go from here?', is 'Not down the slippery slope!'. I believe that we should not cross the line that prohibits altering the human germ line (the genes that are passed on from generation to generation) which making 'three parent babies' would do, or that prohibiting physicians killing their patients or helping them to kill themselves, which allowing euthanasia and physician-assisted suicide permit. Rather, we should stay on the side of each of those lines where neither the crampons nor the skis are needed. But what if we cross them, as the United Kingdom Parliament has just done in legalising 'three biological parent babies' and the Supreme Court of Canada, likewise, in the *Carter* case by legalising 'physician-assisted death'. What if we've been pushed over the edge and are already on the slippery slope?

Then I accept Father Brennan's suggestion to put on the most restricting and protective crampons we can find. I am currently working with others to see how we can, as nearly as possible, realise that outcome in light of the Supreme Court of Canada's judgment in the *Carter* case, which strikes down as unconstitutional the Canadian *Criminal Code* prohibition on assisted suicide and even allows euthanasia in certain circumstances.

But before I comment briefly on the two examples Father Brennan has used to explore the relation of autonomy and the common good, I first want to emphasise and endorse a passage in his lecture. He says:

> It is questionable whether we have enough in our philosophical toolbox when dealing with difficult new social questions if the only instruments available are autonomy, human rights and

non-discrimination. All those involved at the table of public negotiation (regardless of their comprehensive world views, whether religious or not) are entitled to express skepticism about the adequate testing of any new proposal and to seek answers to the likely next steps should the proposal be implemented. They are also entitled to agitate the question whether the proposal is ethically sound according to the diverse ethical views held in the community.

Considerations of autonomy, human rights and non-discrimination are three necessary focuses for testing the validity of state interference through law with individual persons' autonomy, their right to decide for themselves, but they are not sufficient, if we are to ensure that our law and social and public policy are ethical and uphold the important societal values which are required to ensure that future societies are ones in which reasonable people would want to live.

Commonalities

Before commenting on the *Carter* case, I would like to point out the *connecting threads* between the two examples, 'three biological parents babies' and 'physician-assisted suicide and euthanasia', used to illustrate the conflicts that can arise between autonomy and the common good, and the resulting need to prioritise the values in conflict or at least to reasonably accommodate them.

We humans have always formed, upheld and transmitted the most important shared values on which we base our societies around the two great events in each and every human life—birth and death. The choice of pre-birth genetic manipulation and euthanasia as examples of the situations where autonomy and the common good can conflict and we must make values choices, places us in the present-day context in which decisions about the values which should govern birth and death must be made.

Religion used to be the context in which we formed and passed on these values, but that is no longer true in secular Western democracies. Moreover, birth and death have been medicalised and, because everyone relates personally to medicine, it has become an important forum for the formation or destruction of shared societal values in our kind of societies. Because assisted reproductive technologies

(ART's) and euthanasia both involve medicine, both involve societal value formation or destruction.

The involvement of medicine means, however, that we must beware the dangers of the 'medical cloak'. Acts which are seen as ethically unacceptable outside medicine can be seen as acceptable inside it. The white coat of medicine gives a veil of ethical acceptability, because we assume physicians and medicine are ethical. For instance, if we suggest that someone other than a physician—for example, specially trained lawyers or, perhaps, veterinarians, the latter of whom are experts in administering euthanasia—should carry out euthanasia, people are shocked and object strongly, yet it is the same act as the physician performs, which they accept as ethical.

I turn now to look briefly at Father Brennan's two examples.

Making 'three biological parents' babies': Altering the human germ line

The possibility of creating a baby with 'three biological parents' is one of the extraordinary developments in genetics, molecular biology, and assisted reproductive technologies, that face us with values issues and conflicts no humans before us have ever had to confront. The basic issue in employing such world and mind altering technologies is what does respect for human life and human dignity require that we *not* do with them?

What does respect for the transmission of human life require? Is doing so through technological manipulation ever respectful and ethical? Likewise, what does respect for how we treat *in vitro* human embryos demand? Or respect for the resulting 'three-biological-parents' child'? These are historically unprecedented realities. What are the ethics of creating an embryo—transmitting human life—with the intention of killing it in order to use it as a product for the benefit of others, as one method of creating a 'three-biological-parents' child' involves? What are the ethics of altering the human germ line, which always results in inheritable genetic change and changes millions of years of human evolution?

There was almost universal agreement among ethicists that it was unethical to alter the human germ line—that it must be held in trust for future generations as the common heritage of humankind.

Now the United Kingdom Parliament has authorised intentionally intervening to change it. This intervention is different-in-kind, not just different-in-degree from other ART technologies and even from somatic cell gene therapy, because that does not involve inheritable change.

It also validates the ethical acceptability of the creation of 'designer babies', humans whose genetic characteristics did not come about by *chance*—that is, as the philosopher Hans Jonas described it, by having their own unique ticket in the great genetic lottery of the passing on of life—but through another person's *choice*. German philosopher Jürgen Habermas explains creating a human being in that way is wrong because such persons are neither free to construct their own intrinsic identity, because to 'make' themselves requires that they have non-contingent origins, nor are they equal to their designers—the designed is never equal to the designer. In short, their rights both to liberty and to equality, the foundational principles of democracy, are contravened. Moreover, these children are manufactured human beings.

Supporters of 'three parent babies' present a *de minimis* argument for their claims: they say that only 0.01 percent of the child's DNA, thirty-seven out of 20,000 genes, comes from the third parent, so only 2.01 parents, not three parents, are involved. They characterise this intervention as just an incremental addition to other ART procedures we already accept as ethical and legal, and argue that, therefore, it too is ethical. This is an example in a different context of the 'no difference' argument used to support euthanasia. It's also an example of another strategy employed by pro-euthanasia advocates: the use of obfuscating language, which suppresses our moral intuitions and appropriate emotional responses to the intervention in question, both of which can guide us ethically.

Another similarity between the two interventions is that supporters of both 'three parent babies' and euthanasia almost exclusively focus on 'hard', that is heart-wrenching, individual cases, where kindness, compassion and avoidance of suffering are considered to be compelling claims and justifying arguments for the interventions undertaken, and harm—both in the present and, in particular, in the future—to vulnerable individuals, important societal institutions, such as law and medicine, and to society itself, especially some of its most important values, are ignored or denied. In other words, people who argue for allowing 'three parent babies' and euthanasia, both give priority to the value of respect for individual autonomy—to the 'right to choose'—over other competing values and considerations. This focus on choice means the claims of the competent adults who want access to these procedures—a focus on their autonomy and relieving their suffering, whether it arises from an inability to conceive a healthy child or is the result of disease or disability—take centre stage. The other people and entities harmed as a result—the 'common good'—are given little, if any, attention, weight or importance.

Carter case

The *Carter* case provides lessons on what not to do if you don't want physician-assisted suicide or euthanasia legalised by judicial *fiat*, because you believe that would harm both vulnerable people and the common good. I will highlight some of the approaches taken by the Supreme Court of Canada and the issues they raise.

Here's how the Supreme Court framed the issue of whether 'physician-assisted death' should be legally allowed in Canada:

> The question on this appeal is whether the criminal prohibition that puts a person to this [cruel] choice [between taking her own life prematurely, often by violent or dangerous means, or suffering until she dies from natural causes] violates her *Charter* rights to life, liberty and security of the person (s. 7) and to equal treatment by and under the law (s. 15).

The court ruled that it was unnecessary to rule on the issue of discrimination, which was also pleaded by the plaintiffs, because it found the prohibition violated all the section 7 rights—those to life, liberty and security of the person. It did this through the combination of an expansive interpretation of all the section 7 rights, which allowed the court to find that they were all breached, and a very narrow interpretation of what was required to protect the common good, in fact, the elimination of this consideration as a valid objective of the prohibition of assisted suicide, which meant the breaches could not be justified as constitutional under the 'saving provisions' of the Charter.

The court held the *right to life* was breached by an absolute ban on assisted suicide, because a person with a disability would need to commit suicide sooner while still able to do so unaided, than if she could later have assistance in doing so, and consequently her life is shortened by the prohibition. This reasoning converts the right to life to a right to have assistance in committing suicide or even euthanasia, because the court held that the physician may 'provide or administer' the lethal medication. If 'physician-assisted death' includes euthanasia, the Court has converted first degree murder to allowable 'assisted suicide'.

The Court held the *right to liberty* protects a person's freedom to make decisions regarding their own life and body and with respect to medical treatment—it's the right to choose. Quoting the trial judge, the Court held liberty encompasses 'the right to non-interference by the state with fundamentally important and personal medical decision-making' and a dying person who was denied access to 'physician-assisted death' is deprived of this right.

The *right to security of the person*, the Court ruled, is a right to control over one's bodily integrity, the right to be free of suffering or fear of suffering in the future, and this too was breached by the prohibition on assisted suicide.

The Charter's section 7 rights are intended to protect individuals' human rights from breaches by the state, so are necessarily very individualistically based. The state can justify a breach, however, if it shows it was 'in accordance with the principles of fundamental justice' (s. 7) or was such 'as can be demonstrably justified in a free and democratic society' (s. 1). The Court ruled neither of these requirements was fulfilled. The prohibition in being absolute was 'overbroad' in that it restricted people who were not vulnerable who needed 'physician-assisted death' from having access to it and, therefore, was not 'in accordance with the principles of fundamental justice'. And it was not a 'minimal impairment' of section 7 rights needed to protect vulnerable people, so it could not be 'justified in a free and democratic society'.

The court was able to reach the conclusion it did through three main steps in its reasoning, all of which, in my respectful opinion, raise problems. First, at the heart of the *Carter* judgment is what I call the 'no difference' arguments, which are in error when based on false analogies and failures to distinguish between differences of degree and differences of kind, indeed expressly rejecting such distinctions. Second, the court focused on 'preservation of life' as the relevant value against which the harm of striking down an absolute ban on assisted suicide should be tested, instead of what the value of 'respect for life' required if it were to be upheld. And, third, the court accepted several other 'no difference' arguments, including that there is no difference between suicide and assisted suicide, therefore, if suicide is not a crime assisting suicide should not be a crime. So let's look at these steps in more detail.

A major issue in the case was whether 'physician-assisted death' (euthanasia and physician-assisted suicide (E/PAS)) are 'no different' in any ethically relevant way from currently accepted end-of-life treatment decisions, such as refusals of life-support treatment, which result in death. Pro-euthanasia advocates argue there is no difference. Those who are anti-euthanasia believe that there is a 'difference in kind' between caring, relieving pain and suffering and respecting refusals of treatment, on the one hand, and killing, on the other.

Overruling the precedent it set in a previous judgment, the *Rodriguez* case, in which the Supreme Court of Canada expressly rejected the 'no difference' argument, in *Carter* the court accepts and upholds it. It rules there is 'no difference' between refusals of life-support treatment and physician-assisted suicide or, possibly, a lethal injection, therefore, because Canadians accept the former, which the Court characterises as 'passive euthanasia', as ethical and legal, they accept the latter which is 'active euthanasia'. In short, 'physician-assisted death' is found to be simply an incremental addition to interventions Canadians have already accepted. This is a finding by the Court that there is no difference between *allowing a person to die a natural death* and *killing that person*. With respect, I disagree: as has been long recognised, killing is different-in-kind, not just different-in-degree, from justifiably allowing someone to die a natural death. Moreover, the precedents set by justifiable *allowing to die* and legalised *killing* are at opposite ends of a spectrum in terms of their harmful impact on important societal values and on the common good.

The Court also focused on the value of the *preservation of life* and ruled, relying again on the grounds that we accept turning off life-support machines as ethical and legal, that this analogy shows it is not an absolute value, and, therefore, doesn't require an absolute ban on assisted suicide. The Court is correct that preservation of life is not an absolute obligation, but, in my respectful opinion, it's not the most important value to consider in relation to whether or not 'physician-assisted death' should be legalised. Rather, *respect for life* is the value which should have been taken into account, but was not. And the question that should have been, but was not, addressed is what does upholding respect for life at the level of both respect for each individual's life and respect for human life in general at the societal level require that we not do to life? Respect for an individual's life can take into account claims to individual autonomy, but they are not unlimited, because honouring them can harm respect for life at the societal level and maintaining this is an essential component of the common good.

The Supreme Court also ruled that our acceptance of 'allowing to die' shows that the right to life is not a duty to live, and, consequently, 'physician-assisted death' does not contravene the right to life. Rather they held that an absolute ban on assisted suicide contravened the right to life, because a person would be forced to commit suicide earlier while still able to do so without assistance, which means that their life is shortened by the ban.

The Court held, as well, that there was no morally or ethically relevant difference between suicide and assisted suicide and that because suicide is not a crime, assistance in suicide should not be. They also accepted, without considering the issue, that 'physician-assisted death' is medical treatment like any other medical treatments—yet another application of the 'no difference' approach. And they found that there was no difference in terms of the difficulty of preventing the abuse of 'physician-assisted death' and the abuse of other ethically and legally accepted end-of-life treatments.

I propose that the Supreme Court of Canada's acceptance of the argument that there is 'no difference' between 'allowing a person to die' a natural death and killing the person or helping them to kill themselves is not just an incremental change, as pro-euthanasia advocates argue, but a seismic shift in upholding our fundamental value of respect for life.

All state interference with an individual needs justification and, consequently, as Frank Brennan explains, we must undertake at least a threefold assessment by asking in relation to any given interference, such as prohibiting assisted suicide constitutes: Does it respect human rights? Is it non-discriminatory? And is it consistent with the common good? In contrast to the Supreme Court, which answered 'No' to the first question and impliedly to the second, and barely addressed the third, I would answer 'yes' to all of them.

In assessing the risks and harms of legalising 'physician-assisted death', an issue that is at the heart of the common good, the Court found that evidence from the Netherlands and Belgium and five United States states confirmed that 'physician-assisted death' can be controlled with proper regulation which meant there was no evidence of a 'practical slippery slope' (abuse of legalised 'physician-assisted death') or a 'logical slippery slope' (expansion of access to it). The Court refused to reassess the trial judge's findings of fact to these effects or, with the exception of an affidavit by one Belgian expert witness on the abuses occurring in that country, to allow in evidence to show they were wrong, as, with respect, I and others, more knowledgeable than I in this regard, believe them to be. As a result, the judgments threaten the common good, and the human rights of vulnerable people by subjecting them to additional risks and harms, and opening up further possibilities for discrimination against them.

The Court ruled that 'physician-assisted death' posed no exceptional risks to vulnerable people—those who are old, fragile, disabled, mentally ill, depressed, or suicidal—and any such risks can be controlled. They rejected that the ban on assisted suicide had a goal of preservation of life as an object and concluded that the goal was only the narrow one of the protection of vulnerable people in moments of weakness from committing suicide, so with protections for them in place, as they proposed should be the case, an absolute ban was not needed. They did not consider whether upholding 'respect for life' in the interests of the common good required that the ban be maintained.

The Court also held that introducing 'physician-assisted death' would not harm palliative care or the physician-patient relationship; indeed, they remarked that it might improve them. Moreover, they did not require that palliative care must be offered before 'physician-assisted death' could be accessed, an omission that raises issues of respect for human rights, especially the fundamental human right to adequate pain management (see the Declaration of Montreal), discrimination, and harm to the common good in that 'physician-assisted death' will be more likely to be used resulting in its becoming the norm, especially as it will be much less expensive and time-consuming than caring for people who are seriously ill or dying. It's an approach that fails to take into account that the ethical tone of a society is not set by how it treats its strongest, most privileged, most powerful members, but by how it treats those who are weakest, most vulnerable and most in need. Seriously ill and dying people belong in the latter group.

In balancing the values of individual autonomy and respect for life, the Court ruled that individual autonomy—choice—takes priority. They equated having dignity with having control and loss of control with loss of dignity, and dignity as requiring the absence of suffering or even absence of just the anticipation or fear of suffering. Relief of suffering is the overwhelmingly dominant informing principle in the judgment. While that is a worthy and essential goal, serious problems arise when it excludes all other relevant considerations as happens in the *Carter* case. As a result, the judgment focuses almost entirely at the level of individual persons to the exclusion of examining the impact of legalising 'physician-assisted death' on the institutions of medicine or law, or on society and its value'. In short, the judgment constitutes a complete victory for individual autonomy over the common good.

The opening paragraph of the Supreme Court's judgment sets its tone and direction:

> It is a crime in Canada to assist another person in ending her own life. As a result, people who are grievously and irremediably ill cannot seek a physician's assistance in dying and may be condemned to a life of severe and intolerable suffering. A person facing this prospect has two options: she can take her own life prematurely, often by violent or dangerous means, or she can suffer until she dies from natural causes. The choice is cruel.

Those last four words tell us, right at the beginning of its judgment, what the Court will decide in the end. The *Globe and Mail*, one of Canada's national newspapers, had a full, front page photograph the morning after the judgment was released, showing two people, both with their backs to the viewer, one an old person in a wheel chair the other a carer pushing the wheelchair into a long misty corridor. Across the photograph, about a third of the way up, two words were inscribed in very large letters: 'Towards kindness . . . ' By employing the language of cruelty, the court moved to implement kindness through legalising killing.

Chapter 3
Human Rights And The National Interest

The Case study of asylum, migration and national border protection

---

Those of us who live in prosperous, secure countries need to answer the questions: Who has a right to enter my country? What are the preconditions for my government being able decently and fairly to deny a right of entry to someone seeking entry to my country? On my way to Boston, I spent a week in August 2014 down on the Mexico-United States border visiting the KINO Border Initiative at Nogales. I visited the spot at the border fence where Cardinal O'Malley had celebrated mass reaching through the steel girders to give communion to persons on the other side of the border. I heard some of the stories about the desperate attempts of border crossers, many of whom were children fleeing impossibly lawless situations back home heading for the safety of their dreams with relatives already resident in the United States. Fr Sean Carroll SJ, Director of KINO, tells me that the number of people coming to the border has tapered off, in part because of Mexico's southern border plan with Mexican state officials running stricter checkpoints, pulling people off trains and beating them up, and in part because of police activities in countries like Honduras making it more difficult for children to escape. The Mexican southern border plan could not be implemented without US funding. The cumulative effect is 'the externalisation of the US border'.[1]

I am an Australian. Australia is a nation state first founded on Aboriginal dispossession. It is now a very multi-cultural society. It is an island nation continent. It is a nation refounded on migration, and since World War II and the subsequent abolition of the White Australia Policy, on migration from every country on earth. Australia

---

1. Personal communication with Fr Sean Carroll SJ, Director, KINO Border Initiative, Nogales, 2 April 2015.

has a generous, ordered, well policed immigration policy. Australia has been particularly generous receiving refugees fleeing conflicts across the globe, though usually those refugees have been selected by the Australian government issuing visas to those refugees chosen from a large pool. Other refugees have come to Australia on business or tourist visas, then claiming asylum on arrival in Australia. Some refugees have arrived by boat, uninvited and unscreened. Australian Governments of both political persuasions (Liberal and Labor) have expressed a strong preference for the maintenance of an orderly migration program including the reception of an annual quota of refugees chosen from abroad, usually in consultation with the UNHCR. Ever since the first boatloads of Vietnamese asylum seekers arrived in Darwin in 1976, Australian Governments of both political persuasions have had a strong commitment to stopping the boats while at the same time maintaining programs for the resettlement of proven refugees. The Australian public tends to reward political parties which can deliver on the election pledge to stop the boats.

When last at Boston College ten years ago, I worked on a second edition of my book *Tampering with Asylum*. That book and my advocacy made a modest contribution, along with the efforts of many others, to convincing the newly elected Rudd Labor government to wind back the so-called Pacific Solution instituted by the Howard Government in 2001 when boatloads of asylum seekers started arriving in Australian territorial waters from Indonesia. This time these boat people did not originate from Southeast Asia. These asylum seekers came mainly from faraway Afghanistan, Iraq and Iran. They had not fled Indonesia fearing persecution there, but they had continued their global journey from there towards Australia seeking protection, recognition as refugees, and a new life. The measures instituted by the Howard government in 2001 contributed to the changed circumstances which did stop the boats. The reforms instituted by the Rudd government in 2008 contributed to the changed circumstances which resulted in the boats coming in numbers not previously experienced. Commentators like myself were proved wrong. In *Tampering with Asylum*, I had provided a checklist of legal and policy reforms, most of which were enacted by the Rudd government. I had written: 'There is no reason to think that our onshore caseload will increase exponentially given the improved regional arrangements, the virtual offshore border and the tighter controls within Australian territory."[2] During seven years of the Rudd and Gillard Labor governments, over 50,000 asylum seekers arrived by boat. There were at least 1,200 lives lost at sea. By the time the Rudd government was voted out of office, government intelligence sources were advising that the number could rise to 60,000 per annum. For a country of nearly 24 million people with an annual migration intake of 190,000 for skilled migrants and family reunion, with an additional 13,750 places available for humanitarian cases, this was a projected arrival rate which would skew the composition of the migration program very significantly, removing all prospect of offering places to offshore refugees or other persons in desperate humanitarian need.[3] At its most generous in recent years, Australia has provided 20,000 humanitarian places a year. Community groups supportive of refugees have asked government to increase the humanitarian quota to 25,000 per year 'or no less than fifteen per cent of the annual migration intake, whichever is higher'.[4] In 2012, an Expert Panel on Asylum Seekers recommended that Australia increase its humanitarian intake to 27,000 places per annum by 2017. There is a modest Community Proposal Project in place allowing community groups to sponsor up to 500 refugees a year who would not otherwise be chosen to come to Australia. But 500 places are then deducted from the existing annual refugee quota and the visa fees are prohibitive for the most recently arrived refugee groups.

The present humanitarian caseload has been cut by the Abbott government from 20,000 places to a mean 13,750 places. This provides for a minimum of 11,000 places offshore (including up to 1,000 places for women at risk). In 2014–15, 4,400 of these places are going to Syrian and Iraqi refugees. There are over 70,000 processed applications for

---

2. Frank Brennan, *Tampering with Asylum*, second edition (Brisbane: University of Queensland Press, 2007), 261.
3. Of people migrating to Australia, 68 per cent are skilled migrants and thirty-two per cent are from family visa streams. This is further broken down to: skilled migrants: thirty-eight per cent employer sponsored, 34 per cent skilled independent, twenty-two per cent state, territory and regional nominated and six per cent business; family reunion: seventy-nine per cent partner, 14 per cent parent, six per cent child and one per cent other.
4. Australia 21, *Beyond the Boats: Building An Asylum And Refugee Policy For The Long Term*, 2015, 16.

these 11,000 places. Most of these places are for refugees. But there are some places for persons in special humanitarian need who can be sponsored by community members. The remaining allocation is for onshore asylum seekers who entered Australia on a visa having then successfully claimed refugee status. Those asylum seekers arriving without a visa are eligible only for a temporary protection visa should they establish their refugee claim.[5] There are more than 30,000 onshore unvisaed asylum seekers who arrived by boat during the years of the Labor government whose applications for onshore refugee status are still to be processed.

Most of us are citizens of a nation state. It is the nation state primarily which has the duty to protect our human rights. The governments of many nation states have voluntarily ratified an increasing raft of international human rights instruments which in part limit the untrammelled sovereignty of the nation state, providing a framework for enhanced protection of the human rights of all persons within the jurisdiction of the nation state. An international legal order which accords ongoing recognition to national sovereignty is sustainable only if there be an international legal regime ensuring the protection of the human rights of refugees—those whose rights are most flagrantly violated by the government of their own nation state, those who cannot expect any protection from their own government. At the very least, the *quid pro quo* for national sovereignty and the security of national borders is the international community's commitment to protect those who are refugees—those who have fled their home country fearing persecution and abuse of their human rights by their own government. Nation states are entitled to secure their borders but they must not expel their own nationals nor deny their own nationals entry to their country. But what are the moral and legal considerations when it comes to those who are not nationals seeking admission, especially those seeking asylum? Does the asylum seeker have a right to enter? If not, what is the duty of the nation state to the asylum seeker presenting at the border?

Joseph Carens, professor of political science at the University of Toronto, has been a lifetime scholar of the ethics of immigration.

---

5. They may then be eligible for a Safe Haven Enterprise Visa which requires them to move to a rural area for work. In time they might be eligible for a permanent visa.

In 2013 he published a book with that very title, *The Ethics of Immigration*, concluding that 'the conventional view that states are morally entitled to exercise discretionary control over immigration' is wrong. He argues that 'our deepest moral principles require a commitment to open borders (with modest qualifications) in a world where inequality between states is much reduced'.[6] He thinks that our inherited citizenship in rich states like the United States, his home country Canada, and my home country Australia functions as 'a form of illegitimate privilege'.[7] He thinks his ideal would not work the havoc you might imagine if there were greater equality between states as there would then be less incentive for people to leave the state where they grew up and established their roots. But absent that equality, what is to be done?

Carens expresses the fear that there is now 'a deep conflict between what morality requires of democratic states with respect to the admission of refugees and what democratic states and their existing populations see as their interests.'[8] He concedes that the principle of non-refoulement might create disproportionate burdens for rich democratic states all of which design systems for excluding unwelcome applicants. But he rightly insists that this is only a potential problem, not a real one. He notes that 'refugees might reasonably say to themselves that if they have to start life over somewhere new it would be better to do so in a place with more long-term opportunities for themselves and especially for their children. Many refugees would not have the resources to act upon this sort of calculation, but the principle of non-refoulement creates incentives for refugees to seek asylum in a rich democratic state rather than somewhere else'.[9] If rich democratic states were to have an open border policy, no doubt this would become a problem. There is no prospect of any politician who advocates an open border policy being elected in any of these countries. There is no prospect of the Congress or parliament in any of these countries legislating for open borders. Given that the rich democratic states will provide only a limited number of spaces for

---

6. Joseph H Carens, *The Ethics of Immigration* (Oxford: Oxford University Press, 2013), 288.
7. Carens, *The Ethics of Immigration*, 289.
8. Carens, *The Ethics of Immigration*, 223–4.
9. Carens, *The Ethics of Immigration*, 209.

refugees outside their jurisdiction, and given that the limited number of spaces will only ever be a miniscule percentage of those who are *bona fide* refugees in our troubled world, how should those lucky persons in the lottery of resettlement in a rich democratic country be chosen? Carens speaks of the 'moral wrong involved in the use of techniques of exclusion to keep the numbers within bounds' describing 'visa controls, carrier sanctions, and the other techniques of exclusion' as 'indiscriminate mechanisms'. His main suggestion for such democratic countries avoiding the need for the use of these morally questionable techniques is to break the link between claim and place, noting:

> People have incentives to seek asylum in places where they will be better off economically than they were at home, regardless of the strength of their refugee claims. If there were no connection between the place where one requests asylum and the place where one receives protection, however, these incentives would disappear.[10]

Of late, Australian governments have experimented with this approach, denying asylum seekers arriving by boat any prospect of resettlement in Australia, but offering them, on proof of refugee status, resettlement in less desirable countries like Nauru, Papua New Guinea and Cambodia. Most community leaders and advocates regard these experiments as costly, inhumane failures.

On World Refugee Day, 20 June 2014, UNHCR reported 'that the number of refugees, asylum-seekers and internally displaced people worldwide has, for the first time in the post-World War II era, exceeded 50 million people'. 51.2 million people were forcibly displaced at the end of 2013, an increase of more than 6 million on the previous year. In 2014, 866,000 persons applied for asylum in those forty-four industrialised countries which provide UNHCR with statistics. That was a forty-five per cent increase on the previous year. It was the second highest number of annual applications on record. During 2014, more than 218,000 people seeking asylum crossed the Mediterranean Sea seeking access to Europe. That is three times the previous known high of about 70,000 in 2011 during the

---

10. Carens, *The Ethics of Immigration*, 216.

'Arab Spring'. The United States received 121,200 asylum claims, an increase of forty-four per cent on the previous year.

What is to be done when asylum seekers come knocking on our doors in such numbers? Is there a right of entry? If not, what is our obligation to the asylum seeker presenting to officials of our governments whether at our embassies, on the high seas, within our territorial waters, or on our shores? Are we entitled to stipulate a gradation of obligation depending on where an asylum seeker presents? Are we entitled to set up an ante-chamber with an offshore entry door at some considerable distance from our border?

Hiroshi Motomura, the author of the highly acclaimed *Americans in Waiting* has recently published *Immigration Outside the Law*. In part he is investigating how we might extend the rule of law to immigration and border protection, applying the rule of law at the border, inside the border, and after the border crossing. To what extent are our governments justified in excluding the rule of law other than the minimal agreed international safeguards beyond the border? And what are those safeguards? Motomura's main focus is not on asylum seekers outside or at the border but on the 15 million long term residents inside the United States border who are noncitizens without lawful status. He espouses 'a nation with borders, but also a nation committed to a sense of equality and human dignity'[11]—where 'humanitarian obligations recognised by international conventions can override immigration violations'.[12] These ideals have relevance to government behaviour outside the border as well as inside and at the border. Admittedly, the rule of law is more readily applied or invoked when those seeking it already have strong links to the citizenry or a legitimate expectation that they soon will be citizens.

I am honored to be accompanied by Professor Mary Ellen O'Connell who is responding to this paper. I heard her speak at the Society of Christian Ethics Conference in Chicago in January 2015. Here is an international lawyer, passionate about her field of study, principled and unafraid of those who pragmatically urge a yielding to prevailing political realities. Though she does not spend much time focused on issues relating to border protection and the rights of asylum seekers,

---

11. Hiroshi Motomura, *Immigration Outside the Law* (Oxford: Oxford University Press, 2014), 235.
12. Motomura, *Immigration Outside the Law*, 195.

I have every confidence that her critical eye will help bring us back to principled responses to this vexed issue. She may help to correct some of my pessimism about the effectiveness of international law in influencing the laws and policies of rich, democratic countries. In her book *The Power and Purpose of International Law*, she writes:

> International law has deficits, yet it persists as the single, generally accepted means to solve the world's problems. It is not religion or ideology that the world has in common, but international law. Through international law, diverse cultures can reach consensus about the moral norms that we commonly live by. As a result, international law is uniquely suited to mitigate the problems of armed conflict, terrorism, human rights abuse, poverty, disease, and the destruction of the natural environment.[13]

How can international law help us mitigate the problem of human rights abuse when nation states like Australia and the United States are considering how to deal with asylum seekers whether beyond our borders or when presenting at our borders? Mine, I hope, is a principled and pragmatic approach. I invite you to imagine the scene on Saturday, 20 July 2013. I had been in Myanmar out of reach for a week. On the previous afternoon, the Australian Prime Minister Kevin Rudd announced his Papua New Guinea Solution to the increased flow of boat people heading to Australia seeking asylum. He declared that all boat people headed for Australia would be moved to PNG for processing and ultimate resettlement with the guarantee that they would never reach Australia. Landing in Sydney, my first telephone conversation was with Paris Aristotle, a refugee advocate who has been an adviser to Australian governments of all political persuasions. Knowing that I was a friend of Rudd, Paris said to me, 'Frank, you are never to leave the country again without permission.' I then spent a few hours writing a critical assessment of the government proposal publishing it immediately on the internet.[14] I then boarded another plane and flew to Brisbane for a social event at the Prime

---

13. Mary Ellen O'Connell, *The Power and Purpose of International Law*, (Oxford: Oxford University Press, 2011), 14.
14. See 'PNG move proves Australia is not special', http://www.eurekastreet.com.au/article.aspx?aeid=36870.

Minister's home. Being ushered into the Prime Ministerial study, I was able to say that I had already published my view on the new policy. Rudd and I, being friends, agreed that we had our distinctive tasks and duties to perform.

Ever since, I have continued asking what are the ethical and legal preconditions for Australia being able to turn back the boats?[15] Many refugee advocates continue to be upset with me for conceding that any such discussion is theoretically possible, let alone practically necessary. Prime Minister Rudd issued a challenge to all refugee advocates and social justice groups when he appeared on national television in the lead up to the last Australian election saying:

> I think you heard a people smuggler interviewed by a media outlet the other day say that this was a fundamental assault on their business model. Well, that's a pretty gruesome way for him to put that, but the bottom line is this, I challenge anyone else looking at this policy challenge for Australia to deliver a credible alternative policy.
>
> The challenge that I put out to anyone who asks that we should consider a different approach is this: what would you do to stop thousands of people, including children, drowning offshore, other than undertake a policy direction like this? What is the alternative answer?[16]

There is much confusion about the ethical and legal considerations which apply when asylum seekers present at the borders of first world countries. For example, in what, if any, circumstances does or ought an asylum seeker have the right to enter a country not her own in order to seek protection? To be blunt, no asylum seeker should be refouled or sent back to the country where they claim to face persecution unless their claim has been assessed and found wanting; while waiting, no asylum seeker has a right to enter any particular country. In the event that an asylum seeker unlawfully gains access to a country, they should not be penalised for such an unlawful entry or presence provided only that they came in direct flight from the alleged persecution. All lawyers would agree with these blunt

---

15. I first raised the issue earlier at a national summit on asylum issues in June 2013. It is fair to say that the international lawyers were horrified.
16. *Today* program, 23 July 2013.

propositions. Some, especially those schooled in international law, would go further. They would point not just to a country's ratification of the 1951 *Refugees Convention*. They would claim that those countries which have ratified the *Convention against Torture* and the *International Covenant on Civil and Political Rights* cannot refoule an asylum seeker until there has been a determination of any claim that they face torture or 'cruel, inhuman or degrading treatment or punishment'. Some of these lawyers would then take the next leap in human rights protection to assert that all persons have a right to enter any state of their choice provided only they claim to face the risk of persecution, torture, cruel, inhuman or degrading treatment or punishment back home. They translate the right not to be refouled into a right of entry to any state unless and until the state determines that there is no real risk of any of these adverse outcomes either back home or in a transit country. Either the state is able to determine all such claims at the border or else the state must grant entry at least for the purpose of a complete human rights assessment.

Much to the consternation of some refugee advocates, the Australian Government continues to claim: 'International law recognises that people at risk of persecution have a legal right to flee their country and seek refuge elsewhere, but does not give them a right to enter a country of which they are not a national. Nor do people at risk of persecution have a right to choose their preferred country of protection.'[17]

Australian governments (of both political persuasions, Labor and Liberal) have long held the defensible view:

---

17. See http://www.immi.gov.au/media/fact-sheets/61protection.htm. Guy Goodwin Gill says in 'The Right to Seek Asylum: Interception at Sea and the Principle of Non-Refoulement', in *International Journal of Refugee Law*, 23 (2011): 443, 444: 'It is not yet unlawful to move or to migrate, or to seek asylum, even if the criminalisation of 'irregular emigration' by sending states seems to be desired by the developed world. Even so, the range of permissible restrictions on freedom of movement and the absence of any immediately correlative duty of admission, other than towards nationals, make the claim somewhat illusory. Perhaps Article 13(2) of the 1948 Universal Declaration of Human Rights was just a political gesture; perhaps the world today has in fact moved closer to what was then the Soviet position, that the right to freedom of movement should be recognized as *only* exercisable in accordance with the laws of the state.'

The condition that refugees must be 'coming directly' from a territory where they are threatened with persecution constitutes a real limit on the obligation of States to exempt illegal entrants from penalty. In the Australian Government's view, a person in respect of whom Australia owes protection will fall outside the scope of Article 31(1) if he or she spent more than a short period of time in a third country whilst travelling between the country of persecution and Australia, and settled there in safety or was otherwise accorded protection, or there was no good reason why they could not have sought and obtained protection there.[18]

The right to 'seek and enjoy asylum' in the international instruments must be understood as purely permissive. As noted by Justice Gummow of the Australian High Court:

[The] right 'to seek' asylum [in the UDHR] was not accompanied by any assurance that the quest would be successful. A deliberate choice was made not to make a significant innovation in international law which would have amounted to a limitation upon the absolute right of member States to regulate immigration by conferring privileges upon individuals ... Nor was the matter taken any further by the *International Covenant on Civil and Political Rights* ... Article 12 of the *ICCPR* stipulates freedom to leave any country and forbids arbitrary deprivation of the right to enter one's own country; but the *ICCPR* does not provide for any right of entry to seek asylum and the omission was deliberate.[19]

---

18. *Interpreting the Refugees Convention—an Australian Contribution*, Department of Immigration and Multicultural Affairs, Canberra, 2002, 172
19. *MIMA v Ibrahim* [2000] HCA 55, 137–38. Justice Gummow adds, '[I]t has long been recognised that, according to customary international law, the right of asylum is a right of States, not of the individual; no individual, including those seeking asylum, may assert a right to enter the territory of a State of which that individual is not a national ... Over the last 50 years, other provisions of the Declaration have [citing Brownlie] come to 'constitute general principles of law or [to] represent elementary considerations of humanity' and have been invoked by the European Court of Human Rights and the International Court of Justice. But it is not suggested that Art 14 of the UDHR goes beyond its calculated limitation'.

Nation states which are signatories to these international instruments are rightly obliged not to expel peremptorily those persons arriving on their shores, legally or illegally, in direct flight from persecution. That is the limit of the legal obligation. So there may in the future be circumstances in which Australia would be entitled to return safely to Indonesia persons who, when departing Indonesia for Australia, were no longer in direct flight but rather were engaged in secondary movement seeking a more favourable refugee status outcome or a more benign migration outcome. We Australians could credibly draw this distinction if we co-operated more closely with Indonesia providing basic protection and fair processing for asylum seekers there. Until we do that, there is no way of decently stopping the boats.

Thirty-three years ago, United States President Ronald Reagan frustrated by the flow of asylum seekers across the sea from Haiti signed Executive Order 12324 on the 'Interdiction of Illegal Aliens'. Reagan characterised 'the continuing illegal migration by sea of large numbers of undocumented aliens into the southeastern United States' as 'a serious national problem detrimental to the interests of the United States.'

The Oxford don and guru of the international jurisprudence on refugee issues Guy Goodwin-Gill has opined that this Order became 'the model, perhaps, for all that has followed.'[20] I think he is right. Following the military coup in Haiti in 1991, repatriations were suspended for six weeks. Then in May 1992, 'President (George) Bush decided to continue interdiction and repatriation, but without the possibility of screening-in for those who might qualify as refugees.'[21] When inaugurated as President in January 1993, Bill Clinton maintained the interdiction practice, putting paid to the claim that this was just the initiative of the Republicans. It turned out that both major political parties were committed to stopping the boats, doing whatever it takes. Three decades later, it is the same situation in Australia with both sides of politics being committed to stopping the boats. The United States Supreme Court described the matter thus:

---

20. Guy S Goodwin-Gill, 'The Right to Seek Asylum: Interception at Sea and the Principle of Non-Refoulement', in *International Journal of Refugee Law*, 23 (2011): 443.
21. Guy S Goodwin Gill and Jane McAdam, *The Refugee in International Law*, third edition (Oxford: Oxford University Press, 2007), 247.

> With both the facilities at Guantanamo and available Coast Guard cutters saturated, and with the number of Haitian emigrants in unseaworthy craft increasing (many had drowned as they attempted the trip to Florida), the Government could no longer both protect our borders and offer the Haitians even a modified screening process. It had to choose between allowing Haitians into the United States for the screening process or repatriating them without giving them any opportunity to establish their qualifications as refugees. In the judgment of the President's advisers, the first choice not only would have defeated the original purpose of the program (controlling illegal immigration), but also would have impeded diplomatic efforts to restore democratic government in Haiti and would have posed a life-threatening danger to thousands of persons embarking on long voyages in dangerous craft. The second choice would have advanced those policies but deprived the fleeing Haitians of any screening process at a time when a significant minority of them were being screened in.
>
> On May 23, 1992, President Bush adopted the second choice. After assuming office, President Clinton decided not to modify that order; it remains in effect today. The wisdom of the policy choices made by Presidents Reagan, Bush, and Clinton is not a matter for our consideration.[22]

It took fifteen months of concerted advocacy from human rights advocates to convince Clinton to institute refugee status determination interviews on board ship. In *Sale v Haitian Centers Council, Inc*, the United States Supreme Court ruled that these harsh presidential practices were valid. Justice Stevens delivering the opinion of the Court majority said: 'The President has directed the Coast Guard to intercept vessels illegally transporting passengers from Haiti to the United States and to return those passengers to Haiti without first determining whether they may qualify as refugees. The question presented in this case is whether such forced repatriation, "authorised to be undertaken only beyond the territorial sea of the United States"', violates . . . the Immigration and Nationality Act of 1952. We hold that neither (the Act) nor Article 33 of the United Nations Protocol Relating to the Status of Refugees applies to action taken by the Coast

---

22. 509 US 155, 163–6 (1993).

Guard on the high seas.'[23] In relation to Article 33 of the *Refugee Convention*, the Supreme Court said:

> The drafters of the Convention and the parties to the Protocol may not have contemplated that any nation would gather fleeing refugees and return them to the one country they had desperately sought to escape; such actions may even violate the spirit of Article 33; but a treaty cannot impose uncontemplated extraterritorial obligations on those who ratify it through no more than its general humanitarian intent. Because the text of Article 33 cannot reasonably be read to say anything at all about a nation's actions toward aliens outside its own territory, it does not prohibit such actions.[24]

In an uncharacteristic mode for the usually isolationist United States judges, the Supreme Court in footnotes quoted many international law scholars including Guy Goodwin-Gill in support of this proposition. Goodwin-Gill had written: 'A categorical refusal of disembarkation cannot be equated with breach of the principle of *non-refoulement*, even though it may result in serious consequences for asylum-seekers.'[25] They also quoted the respected A Grahl-Madsen who had worked as an in house lawyer for UNHCR for many years. He had written: '*[Non-refoulement]* may only be invoked in respect of persons who are already present—lawfully or unlawfully—in the territory of

---

23. 509 U.S. 155, 158–9 (1993).
24. 509 U.S. 155 , 183.
25. 509 U.S. 155, 184, footnote 41, quoting from Guy Goodwin-Gill, *The Refugee in International Law* (Oxford: Clarendon Press, 1983), 87. Earlier in this work (74–8) Goodwin-Gill concedes, 'At the 1951 Conference, no formal objection appears to have been raised to the Swiss interpretation of non-refoulement, limiting its application to those who have already entered state territory.' He goes on to say, 'Little is to be gained today by any further analysis of the motives of states or the meaning of words in 1951'. He develops his argument saying, 'Let it be assumed that, in 1951, the principle of non-refoulement was binding solely on the conventional level, and that it did not encompass non-rejection at the frontier.' He then argues that state practice has changed and that 'by and large, states in their practice and in their recorded views, have recognised that (non-refoulement) applies to the moment at which asylum-seekers present themselves for entry.' Presumably if state practice can become more accommodating taking on obligations not stipulated in the text, state practice can also become less accommodating confining itself only to those obligations stipulated in the text.

a Contracting State. Article 33 only prohibits the expulsion or return *(refoulement)* of refugees to territories where they are likely to suffer persecution; it does not obligate the Contracting State to admit any person who has not already set foot on their respective territories'[26].

Goodwin-Gill has often pointed out that the *Refugee Convention* has a number of distinct features: as an international text, it must be interpreted in accordance with the general principles of international law; it is 'a 'living instrument' to be interpreted in the light of present day conditions; and it is 'marked by the absence of an in-built monitoring system'.[27] This helps explain why refugee advocates often speak of government policies being contrary to the spirit, if not the letter, of the *Refugee Convention*. That spirit is often enlivened by creative dialogue between UNHCR and the academy. In recent writings Goodwin-Gill has been more critical of those who bluntly espouse that an asylum seeker has no right of entry to a state of his or her choice when in flight from persecution. In his remarks to the 2012 American Society of International Law Conference entitled 'International Norm-Making on Forced Displacement: Challenges and Complexity', he said:

> Although some 148 states are now party to the 1951 Convention and/or the 1967 Protocol, there is no single body with the competence to pronounce with authority on the meaning of words, let alone their application in widely and wildly differentiated and evolving fact situations. In the first instance, it is therefore for each state party to implement its international obligations in good faith and, in its practice and through its courts and tribunals, to determine the meaning and scope of those obligations.[28]

He added:

> Interpreting the 1951 Convention presents the challenge of reconciling a 'living instrument' with consistency with international law. A good-faith interpretation of the treaty

---

26. Goodwin-Gill, *The Refugee in International Law,* 182–3, footnote 40.
27. Guy Goodwin-Gill, 'The Search For The One, True Meaning . . . ', in *The Limits of Transnational Law*, edited by Guy Goodwin-Gill and Helene Lambert (Cambridge: Cambridge University Press, 2010), 204, 206–7.
28. *American Society International Law Proceedings,* 106 (2012): 440.

is called for, which reflects, if not the unknown intent of the drafters, then its object and purpose and the practice of states and their consent to be bound.[29]

Following upon some Australian controversy about whether boat people had a right to enter Australia seeking protection, Goodwin-Gill published a spirited editorial in the *International Journal of Refugee Law* stating:

> The persistent illusion of an absolute, exclusionary competence is still a matter of concern, however, because it tends to frame and direct national legislation and policies in ways that are inimical to international cooperation and, not infrequently, contemptuous of human rights. This persistence is all the more surprising, given what international law has achieved and what international organisation has done to resolve or mitigate humanitarian problems.
>
> ...
>
> The history is important, and no international lawyer can avoid being an historian. This gives us the long view essential to understanding law in the relations of states, and enables us to counter misunderstandings dressed up as advocacy— to point out, for example, that no one in the Commission on Human Rights in 1947–48 ever suggested that a right 'to be granted asylum' (even if it were adopted, which it was not) meant that you could just turn up anywhere by boat and demand and get it. What history tells us, though, is that the French were not without reason to argue that a right to seek asylum would mean little if not linked to a right to be granted asylum. Equally, it shows that other states spoke for their time when responding that this was out of sync with contemporary international law, at least on the narrow, immigration issue of entry and residence. History, then and now, reminds us of the range of legal and practical matters which were left open, and which have since had to be resolved consistently with the general principles of the Declaration at large.
>
> It does not follow, either logically or as a matter of fact, that because states declined to declare a right to be granted asylum in 1948, the individual in flight and at risk of persecution or other relevant harm necessarily has 'no right'

---

29. *American Society International Law Proceedings*, 106 (2012): 442–3.

to enter state territory at any time. The issue is often one of 'framing', for everything depends on context, and the question for international lawyers (and for governments, legislators, critics and commentators) is when and in the light of what obligations might circumstances requiring entry prevail.
...

> Factual scenarios are hugely diverse (which accounts for the difficulty of harmonising refugee decision making across jurisdictions), but it can never be excluded that the state may well be required, as a matter of obligation, to allow an individual to enter its territory for the purpose of protection. To imagine that this is equivalent to granting asylum, as that is understood in the practice of states, is to miss the whole picture—one which is rich in its complexity, demanding more than the simple intonation of words like 'admission', 'entry', 'right', 'no right', without reference to protection and to context and meaning in international law.[30]

In March 2014, Goodwin-Gill followed up with an even more spirited attack on the United States Supreme Court's *Sale* decision:

> Nor do I think that the judgment of the Supreme Court in *Sale* counts for anything juridically significant, other than within the regrettably non-interactive legal system of the United States. Here, the Court ruled for domestic purposes on the construction of the *Immigration and Nationality Act*. What it said on the meaning of the treaty was merely dictum and the Court was not competent—in at least two senses—to rule on international law.
>
> At best, the judgment might constitute an element of State practice, but even here its international relevance can be heavily discounted. The Court failed, among others, to have regard to the binding unilateral statements made by the US when interdiction was first introduced, and the ten years of consistent practice which followed. And as any student of international law will tell you, practice and statements of this nature are highly relevant, particularly when against interest.
>
> UNHCR, moreover, which is responsible for supervising the application of the 1951 Convention/1967 Protocol,

---

30. Guy Goodwin Gill, Editorial: 'The Dynamic of International Refugee Law', in *International Journal of Refugee Law*, 25 (2013): 651, 653–5.

> protested the judgment at the time and has consistently maintained the position set out in its amicus brief to the Supreme Court (and in earlier interventions with the US authorities). Significantly, no other State party to the treaties has objected to UNHCR's position, though the forum and the opportunity are readily available, such as the UNHCR Executive Committee, ECOSOC, or the Third Committee of the UN General Assembly.[31]

Be all this as it may, Goodwin-Gill nonetheless concedes in his most recent writing: 'The 1951 Convention does not deal with the question of admission, and neither does it oblige a state of refuge to accord asylum as such'.[32] Goodwin-Gill's co-author Professor Jane McAdam, when explaining the extra-territorial effect of international obligations and the need for Australian personnel on the high seas to be attentive to the protection needs of asylum seekers before refusing them access to Australian territory, has claimed:

> Only the United States has said that the Refugee Convention does not have that extra-territorial application and that's the basis on which the US justifies its interdiction and expulsion of Haitians and Cubans for instance. The US Supreme Court upheld that view but . . . , to borrow Guy Goodwin-Gill's language, the US Supreme Court was not competent in two senses of the word to rule on the international law obligations of the United States; and in any sense, they were really interpreting a domestic statute. UNHCR at the time and subsequently has spoken out very strongly that the US interpretation is wrong as a matter of international law, and not one country has ever contradicted UNHCR. In international law terms, that is a very strong tacit acceptance that UNHCR's position is correct and that the US is out there on a limb.[33]

---

31. Guy Goodwin-Gill, The Globalization of High Seas Interdiction–Sale's Legacy and Beyond, YLS Sale Symposium, at http://opiniojuris.org/2014/03/16/yale-sale-symposium-globalization-high-seas-interdiction-sales-legacy-beyond/.
32. Guy Goodwin-Gill, 'The International Law of Refugee Protection', in *The Oxford Handbook of Refugee and Forced Migration Studies* (Oxford: Oxford University Press, 2014), 36, 45.
33. Q&A Panel: The High Court and the Asylum Case, Kaldor Centre, University of New South Wales, 22 July 2014, at http://www.kaldorcentre.unsw.edu.au/node/348#overlay-context=events.

I am *ad idem* with Goodwin Gill when he makes the following two observations:

> A State which intercepts a boat carrying refugees on the high sees and which returns them directly to their country of origin violates the principle. Equally, an intercepting State which disembarks refugees and asylum seekers in a country which it knows or reasonably expects will refoule them, or otherwise violate their fundamental human rights, becomes party to that act.

I respectfully part company with his bold generalised assertion that 'non-refoulement is precisely the sort of obligation which is engaged by extraterritorial action'. That is not my understanding of the jurisprudence of the United States Supreme Court. Nor is it my understanding of the jurisprudence of the House of Lords nor of the High Court of Australia. The House of Lords specifically rejected these arguments in relation to non-refoulement and extra-territoriality in 2005.

I am a strong critic, and always have been, of Australian measures such as long term detention, offshore processing such as that practiced in Nauru and Papua New Guinea, and cheque book solutions to resettlement, like the proposed Cambodia solution. Since 2013, knowing there is strong bipartisan support for a return to Pacific solution type options in the Australian Parliament, I have wanted to investigate if ever it might be possible to turn back boats to Indonesia decently, fairly and legally.

The highly respected international lawyers Goodwin Gill and Jane McAdam, seem to be answering, 'No, it could NEVER be legal.' If that be so, it is not an option, and we will be left with non-transparent returns (which suit both Australia AND Indonesia) and punitive, deterrent measures post-entry to Australia and in places like Nauru and PNG.

My quandary has been this. Indonesia is a signatory to the *ICCPR* and *CAT*. It makes regular reports to the requisite United Nations bodies. In 2008, the Committee Against Torture wanted assurances in Indonesian domestic law that refoulement would never be able to occur. But there was no evidence in the report about any particular case or alleged violation. In August 2013, the Human Rights

Committee published its concluding observations on Indonesia. This quite detailed report made no mention of any concerns relating to refoulement—either under *ICCPR* or *CAT*. The question arises: Given that Indonesia is a signatory to *CAT* and *ICCPR*, given that Indonesia complies with the reporting provisions of *CAT* and *ICCPR*, given that there are no confirmed reports of Indonesia wrongly refouling persons returned from Australia, and given that Indonesia is NOT and is not likely to be a signatory to the *Refugee Convention*, could the conditions ever be fulfilled which would warrant Australia returning asylum seekers to Indonesia provided only that Australia is satisfied that the asylum seekers are not in direct flight from persecution IN Indonesia, and provided Australia is satisfied that the returnees will not face the real risk of torture, cruel or degrading treatment in Indonesia?

It is the height of legal formalism to posit that one could never entertain the notion of setting preconditions for such returns (such as UNHCR supervised processing and IOM administered accommodation and services etc) only because Indonesia is not a signatory to the *Refugee Convention*. It is one thing to have credible evidence of wrongful refoulement from Indonesia prior to determination of claims; it is another to rule out *ab initio* the possibility of safe returns to Indonesia. If you do the latter, how could you ever ever be satisfied that Indonesia's accession to the *Refugee Convention* would justify returns? The *reductio ad absurdum* of Goodwin Gill's position is that Australia could NEVER return anyone to Indonesia regardless of what instruments it had signed and regardless of what international reporting it had undertaken.

Many of the Australian debates now come down to advocates alleging that Australian policy is contrary to the 'spirit' of the *Refugee Convention*, with government responding that its policy is consistent with the 'letter' of the Convention. Compliance with the 'letter' does not make a policy right or decent. There is often a need for more robust moral argument and also more finely honed constitutional and statutory construction arguments to counter what is being proposed.

Whatever of United States exceptionalism in international law, the United States approach has in fact given licence and a paradigm these last two decades to other rich nations worried about an influx of boat people. Australian governments of both political persuasions have adopted the jurisprudence of the United States Supreme Court, and to date the Australian High Court has not begged to differ. In 2005, the House of Lords indicated its agreement with the United States Supreme Court decision and reasoning about Article 33. In *Regina (European Roma Rights Centre and others)* v *Immigration Officer at Prague Airport,* the House of Lords had been asked to rule that the US decision was wrong. The House of Lords not only declined. Their Lordships having surveyed the history of the 1951 Convention and later attempts to amend or re-interpret it, stated categorically that the non-refoulement provision related only to persons within the territory of a state. They considered all the arguments for expansion of the non-refoulement principle to beyond the frontier of the nation state. Goodwin-Gill appeared as counsel for UNHCR submitting that 'the principle of non-refoulement and non-rejection at the frontier is a rule of customary international law, operating in parallel and co-existing with treaty rules (relevantly, article 33 of the *Refugee Convention*) which obliges states not to return refugees to territories where they risk persecution, torture or death, and not to reject such a person at the frontier of their country of nationality where they fear persecution'. UNHCR's argument was rejected by the House of Lords. In the lead judgment in the House of Lords, Lord Bingham stated:

> In 1967 the United Nations adopted a Declaration on Territorial Asylum which provided, in article 3, that no person entitled to invoke article 14 of the Universal Declaration of Human Rights should be subjected to measures such as rejection at the frontier, but a conference held in 1977 to embody this and other provisions in a revised convention ended in failure. As Justice Gummow (of the Australian High Court) put it in *Ibrahim*, in his judgment given in October 2000, 'there have been attempts which it is unnecessary to recount here to broaden the scope of the Convention itself by a Draft United Nations Convention on Territorial Asylum but these collapsed more than twenty years ago.'[34]

Lord Bingham concluded the discussion about the submission urging the court to expand the principle of non-refoulement to persons at

---

34. [2005] 2 AC 1 at 30.

the frontier and outside the territory of the nation state signatory to the Convention:

> In considering whether the rule contended for has received the assent of the nations, it is pertinent to recall that the states parties to the 1951 Convention have not, despite much international discussion, agreed to revise its terms or extend its scope at any time since 1967. None of the citations (put in support of the proposition) is from a legislative instrument. The House was referred to no judicial decision supporting the rule contended for and a number of recent decisions (*Sale* in the United States, *Ibrahim* and *Khawar* in Australia) are inimical to it. Have the states in practice observed such a rule? It seems to me clear that they have not.[35]

Whereas other law lords said they simply agreed with Lord Bingham on the asylum issues raised, Lord Hope of Craighead dealt with the questions himself and was even more forthright. He said:

> I do not, with respect, think that the *Sale* case was wrongly decided. The issue in that case was not as to what was or was not fair. The majority recognised the moral weight of the argument that a nation should be prevented from repatriating refugees to their potential oppressors whether or not the refugees were within that nation's borders. But in their opinion both the text and the negotiating history of article 33 affirmatively indicated that it was not intended to have extraterritorial effect. Judicial support for this view is found in the opinion of Gummow J (of the Australian High Court) in *Applicant A v Minister for Immigration and Ethnic Affairs* (1997) and in the other authorities which Lord Bingham has referred to.[36]

One wonders what is the point of UNHCR putting submissions to the High Court of Australia as they did in October 2014 proposing that 'the weight of opinion at international law is that the principle of non-refoulement, including under Art 33 (1) of the *Refugee Convention* applies, wherever a State exercises jurisdiction, and whether it

---

35. [2005] 2 AC 1 at 38.
36. [2005] 2 AC 1 at 54.

is exercised *de jure* or *de facto*. The UNHCR is only aware of one superior court decision that is inconsistent with this understanding, being the decision of the United States Supreme Court in *Sale*.[37] Both the Australian High Court and the House of Lords have in the past followed the Supreme Court in *Sale* or at least assumed it is correct. The UNHCR submission was misleading and unhelpful, especially given that UNHCR had been an intervener in the House of Lords case.[38] For its part, the Australian Human Rights Commission submitted to the High Court 'that the construction given to Article 33(1) by the majority of the US Supreme Court in *Sale* v *Haitian Centers Council Inc* is incorrect'.[39] In its recent decision *CPCF* v

---

37. UNHCR, Written Submissions, *CPCF v Minister for Immigration and Border Protection*, No S169 of 2014, 15 September 2014, 9.
38. Counsel for the Commonwealth was able to deal with the matter simply and forthrightly in oral argument: 'Your Honours, I will not take you to *Sale* or the *Roma Rights Case*, but it was argued in the *Roma Rights Case* in the House of Lords that *Sale* was wrong and that invitation was rejected expressly in the judgment of Lord Hope. The leading judgment was given by Lord Bingham but at the end of his judgment, Lord Bingham agreed with Lord Hope's remarks. It was, we submit, the whole House of Lords rejected the submission that *Sale* was wrong and we submit your Honours should not lightly conclude that the highest courts in both the United States and the United Kingdom were wrong in the conclusion that they reached.'
(available at http://www.austlii.edu.au/au/other/HCATrans/2014/228.html)
39. Australian Human Rights Commission, Proposed Submissions, *CPCF v Minister for Immigration and Border Protection*, High Court of Australia, 11 September 2014, 8. The AHRC submission provides a novel, expansive approach to the historic interpretation of Article 33 when it states at 3: 'According to Goodwin-Gill and McAdam, the first reference in an international agreement to the principle that refugees should not be returned to their country of origin occurred in the 1933 Convention relating to the International Status of Refugees. Article 3 of that Convention contained an undertaking by States not to remove resident refugees or keep them from their territory "by application of police measures, such as expulsions or non-admittance at the frontier (refoulement)" unless dictated by national security or public order. The language that ultimately formed the basis for Article 33(1) of the Refugees Convention was the product of an *Ad hoc* Committee on Statelessness and Related Problems appointed by the United Nations Economic and Social Council. A representative of the United States delegation on that Committee provided the following description of the key principle: 'Whether it was a question of closing the frontier to a refugee who asked admittance, or of turning him back after he had crossed the frontier, or even of expelling him after he had been admitted to residence in the territory, the problem was more or less the same . . . Whatever the case may be . . . he must

Minister for Immigration and Border Protection, the High Court of Australia did not cast any adverse imputations on the relevant United States and United Kingdom decisions. In this case, the High Court found no grounds for invalidating the Australian government's holding of 157 Tamil asylum seekers on an Australian vessel on the high seas in the Indian Ocean for a month while Australia attempted to negotiate their return to India from whence they had set sail. The Chief Justice, referring to the United States and United Kingdom decisions, said, 'The defendants argued that the non-refoulement obligation under the *Refugees Convention* only applied to receiving States in respect of refugees within their territories. There is support for that view in some decisions of this Court, the House of Lords and the Supreme Court of the United States.'[40] Justice Keane referring to those decisions, said, 'Judicial authority in Australia, the United Kingdom and the United States of America suggests that a state's obligations under the Convention arise only with respect to persons who are within that state's territory.'[41] He went on to say, 'Under the *Migration Act,* the protection obligations imposed on the Executive government are afforded to non-citizens who are within Australian territory. The authorities suggest that this limitation is consistent with the circumstance that the protection obligations imposed by the Convention concern rights to be afforded to persons within the territory of Contracting States.'[42]

The European Court of Human Rights has developed a more human-rights-friendly approach to the reception of asylum seekers. In the future the Australian High Court might be convinced to follow more the jurisprudence of the European Court of Human Rights rather than the United States Supreme Court and the United Kingdom Supreme Court, at least when interpreting Australian statutes which are arguably consistent with the fulfillment of Australia's international treaty obligations. But this would require the High Court to abandon some of its own earlier jurisprudence as well as the House of Lords'

---

  not be turned back to a country where his life or freedom could be threatened.'"
40. CPCF v *Minister for Immigration and Border Protection* [2015] HCA 1, [10].
41. CPCF v *Minister for Immigration and Border Protection* [2015] HCA 1, [461]. He did go on to observe, 'The plaintiff does not accept that this body of authority is correct, but it is unnecessary to come to a conclusion on that point.'
42. CPCF v *Minister for Immigration and Border Protection* [2015] HCA 1, [492].

unequivocal endorsement of the United States Supreme Court's approach. What makes this most unlikely is that the Australian parliament is legislating exhaustive provisions which are dismissive of international law. In the absence of any Australian bill of rights or *Human Rights Act*, the High Court of Australia is then constrained to interpret the unambiguous Australian statutory provisions regardless of the letter or spirit of international instruments and law. As Justice Keane said in the recent case:

> Australian courts are bound to apply Australian statute law 'even if that law should violate a rule of international law'. International law does not form part of Australian law until it has been enacted in legislation. In construing an Australian statute, our courts will read 'general words . . . subject to the established rules of international law' unless a contrary intention appears from the statute. In this case, there is no occasion to invoke this principle of statutory construction. The terms of the Act are specific. They leave no doubt as to its operation.[43]

All seven judges of the High Court basically took this approach. The Australian parliament has been so specific in codifying the law of asylum at the frontier that there is nothing for the judges to do except apply the letter of the law, regardless of the general principles of international law. You may just as well be quoting the *Catechism of the Catholic Church* to them, as be submitting the learned opinions of international lawyers.

In Europe, the focus has been on boats coming across the Mediterranean Sea. The European Court of Human Rights became apprised of the European Union practices in the Mediterranean in the 2012 case *Hirsi* v *Italy*[44]. The applicants in that case were eleven Somali nationals and thirteen Eritrean nationals who were part of a group of about two hundred individuals who left Libya aboard three vessels with the aim of reaching the Italian coast. On 6 May 2009, when the vessels were 35 nautical miles south of the island of Lampedusa, they were intercepted by three ships from the Italian Revenue Police and the Coastguard. The occupants of the intercepted vessels were

---

43. *CPCF* v *Minister for Immigration and Border Protection* [2015] HCA 1, [462].
44. Available at http://hudoc.echr.coe.int/sites/eng/pages/search.aspx?i=001-109231.

transferred onto Italian military ships and returned to Tripoli. On arrival in the Port of Tripoli, the migrants were handed over to the Libyan authorities. According to the applicants' version of events, they objected to being handed over to the Libyan authorities but were forced to leave the Italian ships. At a press conference held on 7 May 2009 the Italian Minister of the Interior stated that the operation to intercept the vessels on the high seas and to push the migrants back to Libya was the consequence of the entry into force on 4 February 2009 of bilateral agreements concluded with Libya, and which represented an important turning point in the fight against clandestine immigration. The applicants complained that they had been exposed to the risk of torture or inhuman or degrading treatment in Libya and in their respective countries of origin as a result of having been returned. They relied on Article 3 of the European Convention on Human Rights which provides: 'No one shall be subjected to torture or to inhuman or degrading treatment or punishment.'

The Court said:

> The Court has already had occasion to note that the States which form the external borders of the European Union are currently experiencing considerable difficulties in coping with the increasing influx of migrants and asylum seekers. It does not underestimate the burden and pressure this situation places on the States concerned, which are all the greater in the present context of economic crisis. It is particularly aware of the difficulties related to the phenomenon of migration by sea, involving for States additional complications in controlling the borders in southern Europe. However, having regard to the absolute character of the rights secured by Article 3, that cannot absolve a State of its obligations under that provision. The Court reiterates that protection against the treatment prohibited by Article 3 imposes on States the obligation not to remove any person who, in the receiving country, would run the real risk of being subjected to such treatment.[45]

The Court ruled unanimously that the applicants were within the jurisdiction of Italy for the purposes of Article 1 of the Convention;

---

45. Available at http://hudoc.echr.coe.int/sites/eng/pages/search.aspx?i=001-109231, para 122.

that there had been a violation of Article 3 of the Convention on account of the fact that the applicants were exposed to the risk of being subjected to ill-treatment in Libya; and that there had been a violation of Article 3 of the Convention on account of the fact that the applicants were exposed to the risk of being repatriated to Somalia and Eritrea.[46]

When Lord Neuberger, the Chief Justice of the United Kingdom, visited Australia in 2014, he took the opportunity to express some forthright views about the European Court of Human Rights. He told the justices of the Victorian Supreme Court:

> I think we may sometimes have been too ready to treat Strasbourg court decisions as if they were determinations by a UK court whose decisions were binding on us. It is a civilian court under enormous pressure, which sits in chambers far more often than in banc, and whose judgments are often initially prepared by staffers, and who have produced a number of inconsistent decisions over the years. I think that we are beginning to see that the traditional common law approach may not be appropriate, at least to the extent that we should be more ready not to follow Strasbourg chamber decisions.[47]

---

46. In a separate judgment, Judge Pinto de Albuquerque joined issue with the US Supreme Court. He said: 'It is true that the statement of the Swiss delegate to the conference of plenipotentiaries that the prohibition of *refoulement* did not apply to refugees arriving at the border was supported by other delegates, including the Dutch delegate, who noted that the conference was in agreement with this interpretation. It is also true that Article 33 § 2 of the United Nations Refugee Convention exempts from the prohibition of *refoulement* a refugee who constitutes a danger to the security of a country 'in which he is' and refugees on the high seas are in no country. One might be tempted to construe Article 33 § 1 as containing a similar territorial restriction. If the prohibition of *refoulement* were to apply on the high seas, it would create a special regime for dangerous aliens on the high seas, who would benefit from the prohibition, while dangerous aliens residing in the country would not.
    'With all due respect, the United States Supreme Court's interpretation contradicts the literal and ordinary meaning of the language of Article 33 of the United Nations Refugee Convention and departs from the common rules of treaty interpretation.'
47. Conference of the Judges of the Supreme Court of Victoria, 8 August 2014, available at http://supremecourt.uk/docs/speech-140808.pdf.

But in the end, he came down in favour of the general approach of the European Court, conceding that the United Kingdom's ratification of the Convention and the passage of its own *Human Rights Act* resulted in the courts being 'pitchforked into ruling on the most contentious issues of the day' including asylum seekers' rights. He observed:

> The fact that 'unelected' judges, especially foreign judges, are perceived to have been given powers which they previously had not enjoyed, coupled with the distaste in some political quarters for all things European, and the media's concentration on prisoners' votes and asylum seekers, has rendered the Convention something of a whipping boy for some politicians and newspapers. This appears to many people to be unfortunate. There are decisions of the Strasbourg court with which one can reasonably disagree, indeed with which I disagree. This is scarcely surprising; indeed, it would be astonishing if it were otherwise. However, to my mind, there are very few of its decisions which can fairly be said to be misconceived.

Australia does not have a *Human Rights Act*, and it is not accountable to any outside judicial body like Strasbourg. This may help to account for Australia's less nuanced approach to 'stopping the boats'. In Australia, the Executive finds itself freer from judicial constraint. Mind you, the Australian High Court flexes its muscle from time to time. In September 2014, the court unanimously struck down the government's attempt to avoid giving permanent protection visas to asylum seekers proven to be refugees who also pass the requisite health and security checks.[48] But since then the Parliament has legislated to provide only temporary protection visas.

---

48. *Plaintiff S4-2014* v *Minister for Immigration and Border Protection* [2014] HCA 34 (11 September 2014). The plaintiff had no visa permitting him to enter or remain in Australia. On arrival in Australia, at Christmas Island, the plaintiff was lawfully taken into immigration detention where he was held for two years while being assessed for a protection visa. The department determined that the plaintiff was 'grant ready'. 'That is, the department determined that the plaintiff was a refugee and satisfied relevant health and character requirements for the grant of a protection visa.' The Minister then decided not to grant a protection visa but rather another short term visa which would then preclude the grant of a permanent protection visa. The Court ruled that the grant of this visa was invalid as its grant would have undermined the whole legislative purpose of the two year

Australia is presently quite sterile ground for international lawyers agitating the rights of asylum seekers. Not only has the High Court made clear that there is little room for the application of international law when interpreting tight statutory provisions aimed at enhancing border protection. The Australian Parliament has now legislated a string of new statutory provisions specifying that the exercise of various border protection powers is not invalid:

> (a) because of a failure to consider Australia's international obligations, or the international obligations or domestic law of any other country; or
> (b) because of a defective consideration of Australia's international obligations, or the international obligations or domestic law of any other country; or
> (c) because the exercise of the power is inconsistent with Australia's international obligations.[49]

The Australian Executive has displayed its frustration with the international law approach as enunciated by United Nations agencies, with the Prime Minister Tony Abbott responding to criticisms by the UN Special Rapporteur on Torture, Juan Mendez, who had expressed criticisms of Australia's offshore asylum arrangements, admitting that he had not visited the facilities. The Rapporteur tabled at the United Nations Human Rights Council a series of broad sweeping findings against Australia in relation to torture et al. For example in relation to one complaint, Mendez wrote:

> In the absence of information to the contrary, the Rapporteur concludes that there is substance in the allegations presented in the initial communication, reiterated above, and thus, that the Government of Australia, by failing to provide adequate detention conditions; end the practice of detention of children; and put a stop to the escalating violence and tension at the Regional Processing Centre, has violated the right of the asylum seekers, including children, to be free from torture

---

detention, namely assessment for a permanent protection visa.
49. s. 22A *Maritime Powers Act 2013*, inserted by s. 6, *Migration and Maritime Powers Legislation Amendment (Resolving the Asylum Legacy Caseload) Act 2014*.

or cruel, inhuman or degrading treatment, as provided by articles 1 and 16 of the CAT.[50]

Suggestions to the United Nations Human Rights Council that a government is torturing children do need more than the repetition of hearsay allegations. Prime Minister Abbott said:

> I really think Australians are sick of being lectured to by the United Nations, particularly, particularly given that we have stopped the boats, and by stopping the boats, we have ended the deaths at sea. The most humanitarian, the most decent, the most compassionate thing you can do is stop these boats because hundreds, we think about 1200 in fact, drowned at sea during the flourishing of the people smuggling trade under the former government ... I think the UN's representatives would have a lot more credibility if they were to give some credit to the Australian government for what we've been able to achieve in this area.[51]

On the issue of border protection and asylum, it has reached the stage in Australia that government and the parliament are attempting to lock out all influence by international law.

Having offered some observations about the present *cul de sac* confronting international lawyers concerned about Australia's behaviour at the border, I now turn to the effects of religious discourse and other moral urgings in the public square, convinced that such discourse can often augment, consolidate and extend the protection of the human rights of those whose interests do not coincide with those of the majority in a nation state.

Permit me to be so bold, being a Jesuit and a lawyer, to suggest that public moral argument posited on religious conviction and domestic judicial review are two necessary, additional devices for reining in the executive government responding to populist sentiment to secure the borders and stop the boats. It is the judicial method which permits fine consideration of the claims of those who present at our borders, helping to counter the more broad stroke governmental decisions to

---

50. Juan E Méndez, Report of the Special Rapporteur on torture and other cruel, inhuman or degrading treatment or punishment, A/HRC/28/68/Add.1, 6 March 2015, p 8.
51. *Sydney Morning Herald*, 9 March 2015.

punish those who present at our borders in order to send a message to other intending asylum seekers and to give a preference to those asylum seekers chosen by government rather than those who self-select by presenting themselves at the border. It is the moral argument (whether religious or not) which augments the secular liberal approach within the nation state. The secular liberal finds it hard to formulate an argument for universal care extending beyond the injunction for government to care for their own citizens maintaining the security of their borders. At the very least, the secular liberal should concede the assistance which might be obtained from the religious practitioners who profess the dignity of all human persons, and not just those holding passports for nation states living in peace and with economic security.

Marking the 60th anniversary of the United Nations Declaration of Human Rights, the late and revered Seamus Heaney wrote:

> Since it was framed, the Declaration has succeeded in creating an international moral consensus. It is always there as a means of highlighting abuse if not always as a remedy: it exists instead in the moral imagination as an equivalent of the gold standard in the monetary system. The articulation of its tenets has made them into world currency of a negotiable sort. Even if its Articles are ignored or flouted—in many cases by governments who have signed up to them—it provides a worldwide amplification system for the 'still, small voice'.[52]

Religious leaders have a capacity to contribute to that amplification of the still, small voice, as of course do international lawyers. So too do poets, folk singers, and novelists. The concept of human rights has real work to do whenever those with power justify their solutions to social ills or political conflicts only on the basis of majority support or by claiming the solutions will lead to an improved situation for the mainstream majority. Even if a particular solution is popular or maximises gains for the greatest number of people, it might still be wrong and objectionable. There is a need to have regard to the wellbeing of all members of the human community, and not just those within the preferred purview of government consideration.

---

52. *Irish Times*, 10 September 2009.

Lampedusa continues to be a beacon for asylum seekers fleeing desperate situations in Africa seeking admission into the European Union. Lampedusa is a lightning rod for European concerns about the security of borders in an increasingly globalised world where people as well as capital flow across porous borders. That's why Pope Francis went there on his first official papal visit outside Rome. At Lampedusa on 8 July 2013, Pope Francis said:

> 'Where is your brother?' Who is responsible for this blood? In Spanish literature we have a comedy of Lope de Vega which tells how the people of the town of Fuente Ovejuna kill their governor because he is a tyrant. They do it in such a way that no one knows who the actual killer is. So when the royal judge asks: 'Who killed the governor?', they all reply: 'Fuente Ovejuna, sir'. Everybody and nobody! Today too, the question has to be asked: Who is responsible for the blood of these brothers and sisters of ours? Nobody! That is our answer: It isn't me; I don't have anything to do with it; it must be someone else, but certainly not me. Yet God is asking each of us: 'Where is the blood of your brother which cries out to me?' Today no one in our world feels responsible; we have lost a sense of responsibility for our brothers and sisters. We have fallen into the hypocrisy of the priest and the levite whom Jesus described in the parable of the Good Samaritan: we see our brother half dead on the side of the road, and perhaps we say to ourselves: 'poor soul . . . !', and then go on our way. It's not our responsibility, and with that we feel reassured, assuaged. The culture of comfort, which makes us think only of ourselves, makes us insensitive to the cries of other people, makes us live in soap bubbles which, however lovely, are insubstantial; they offer a fleeting and empty illusion which results in indifference to others; indeed, it even leads to the globalisation of indifference. In this globalised world, we have fallen into globalised indifference. We have become used to the suffering of others: it doesn't affect me; it doesn't concern me; it's none of my business!
>
> Here we can think of Manzoni's character—'the Unnamed'. The globalization of indifference makes us all 'unnamed', responsible, yet nameless and faceless.[53]

---

53. Available at http://w2.vatican.va/content/francesco/en/homilies/2013/documents/papa-francesco_20130708_omelia-lampedusa.html.

It is all very well for the pope to say these things. But who is listening? And even if they are listening, who is taking any notice? Should anyone other than Catholics bother taking any notice? The pope's intervention and the innate moral sense of the Italian community that there had to be a more decent way of dealing with prospective migrants drowning in the Mediterranean contributed to the Italian Government's decision to establish the *Mare Nostrum* operation.

Recently in Australia, two of our greatly admired ex-prime ministers from opposite sides of the political fence have died. They were Gough Whitlam and Malcolm Fraser. Whitlam was prime minister at the end of the Vietnam War. He was succeeded by Fraser in December 1975. Each of them was concerned by the prospect of large numbers of Vietnamese refugees arriving in Australia by boat and without visas. Their political parties were equally committed to stopping the boats. Initially with the fall of South Vietnam, Australian politicians and civil servants were very wary about receiving large numbers of refugees from Vietnam. A joint parliamentary committee was unanimously of the view when reporting in 1976 that prior to the evacuation of the Australian embassy in Saigon in 1975 there was 'deliberate delay in order to minimise the number of refugees with which Australia would have to concern itself'.[54] Politicians from both sides of the aisle stated, 'As unpalatable as it may be, we are forced to conclude that the [Whitlam] Government acted reluctantly and, as expressed by one witness, in order to placate an increasingly suspicious Australian public.'[55]

As Prime Minister, Fraser gave great leadership in the Australian community cultivating public acceptance of the idea that Australia would play its part in receiving a significant number of Vietnamese refugees chosen by Australian government officials from camps in other South East Asian countries like Thailand. Eventually an orderly departure program was negotiated with the Vietnamese government. On both sides of the political aisle in Australia, there were concerns expressed about 'queue jumpers' and those falsely claiming to be refugees while seeking a better life. Both Whitlam and Fraser, like

---

54. *Australia and the Refugee Problem*, Report from the Senate Standing Committee on Foreign Affairs and Defence, Parliamentary Paper 329/1976, 1 December 1976, 24.
55. *Australia and the Refugee Problem*, 25.

all their political successors, expressed concerns about boat people arriving without visas and without prior selection by Australian officials. In May 1977, Fraser's Minister for Immigration, Michael MacKellar set out Australia's first comprehensive refugee policy insisting: 'The decision to accept refugees must always remain with the Government of Australia.'[56] He announced, 'There will be a regular intake of Indo-Chinese refugees from Thailand and nearby areas at a level consistent with our capacity as a community to resettle them. In this operation we shall be relying greatly on the co-operation of the UNHCR, other Governments, especially the Thai Government, and voluntary agencies in Australia.'[57] A year later, there was an increasing flow of refugees out of Vietnam and into camps around South East Asia. The Fraser government insisted on the need for a co-operative international approach. When non-government agencies started to provide assistance to boat people on the high seas, MacKellar told parliament: 'I put the proposition that the people concerned with the project could not see a situation emerging where Australia would automatically allow the entry of any people that such a vessel happened to pick up.'[58] On 29 June 1978, the Labor Party's spokesman on immigration matters, Dr Moss Cass, wrote a very inflammatory opinion piece in *The Australian* lamenting the arrival of over 1,000 boat people in Darwin Harbour, none of whom had been sent back to Vietnam. He said, 'The implications of a government policy which accepts queue jumping on this scale are obvious.' He was adamant that 'those refugees seeking residence in Australia who jump the queue by arriving on our shores without proper authorisation should not be given resident status, even temporarily'. On 15 August 1978, the Labor frontbencher Clyde Cameron who had been Whitlam's Immigration Minister asked Prime Minister Malcolm Fraser a rather hostile and insinuating question: 'Will he tell the Parliament what approaches were made by the United States of America which were in any way responsible for the decision to permit Vietnamese nationals to enter Australia without permits.' Fraser answered:

---

56. House of Representatives, *Hansard*, 24 May 1977, 1714.
57. House of Representatives, *Hansard*, 24 May 1977, 1716.
58. House of Representatives, *Hansard*, 7 June 1978, 3149.

> The United States of America has not attempted to influence procedures for entry to Australia. The Australian Government will at all times decide the requirements for entry to Australia. No Vietnamese nationals are permitted to enter Australia without entry permits. The 1634 boat refugees who have arrived in Darwin without prior authority were issued with temporary entry permits on arrival pending consideration of their applications to remain here.[59]

The major political parties were agreed on the need to arrest the flow of boats, while being generous with the resettlement of Vietnamese refugees who then came through the camps in South East Asia under what later became the comprehensive plan of action in 1989. On 16 March 1982, Ian McPhee, Fraser's next Immigration Minister after MacKellar, provided Parliament with an update on the government's refugee policy restating, 'The decision to accept refugees must always remain with the Australian Government'. He told Parliament:

> During my visit last year I reached the conclusion, commonly held by many involved in both the Indo-Chinese and Eastern European refugee situations, that a proportion of people now leaving their homelands were doing so to seek a better way of life rather than to escape from some form of persecution. In other words their motivation is the same as over one million others who apply annually to migrate to Australia. To accept them as refugees would in effect condone queue-jumping as migrants.[60]

He called for a balance between compassion and realism. He announced progress with an orderly departure program aimed at arresting the flow of boats out of Vietnam. He reached agreement with his counterparts in Thailand and Malaysia how to arrest the flow and how to handle the numbers coming through. All this humanitarian effort was posited on the premise of stopping the boats coming uninvited to Australia.

There was a very moving scene at the recent state funeral of Malcolm Fraser when Vietnamese Australians thronged outside the church carrying placards which read: 'You are forever in our hearts:

---

59. House of Representatives, *Hansard*, 12 September 1978, 902.
60. House of Representatives, *Hansard*, 16 March 1982, 991.

farewell to our true champion of humanity: Malcolm Fraser'. I honour Fraser, but not because he opened our borders to fleeing boat people coming in their tens of thousands. He didn't. He secured the borders, and then he led the nation in opening 'our arms and hearts to tens of thousands of refugees' as the novelist Tim Winton put it. Winton is wrong to claim that Fraser welcomed the boats. Winton is right to proclaim:

> I was proud of my country, then, proud of the man who made it happen, Malcolm Fraser, whose greatness shames those who've followed him in the job. Those were the days when a leader drew the people up and asked the best of them and despite their misgivings, Australians rose to the challenge. And I want to honour his memory today.

Seeking the right balance between compassion and realism, between the human rights of asylum seekers and the national interest of a rich democratic country, we might find as much guidance from the memory of the last generation of refugees in their honouring of the last generation of political leaders who tried to forge a solution compassionate and fair to the many who were seeking asylum and acceptable to the voting public. In a country like Australia, I have concluded that stopping the boats is a precondition to finding a politically acceptable, compassionate and fair solution. The boats will be stopped. But they need to be stopped decently and fairly so that the community might then be encouraged and led to be more generous in opening the doors to a higher quota of refugees each year being selected by government from situations of acute despair, and in funding the international agencies and other governments caring for asylum seekers in transit. As one of the richest, most democratic countries in Southeast Asia, Australia will always be an attractive destination for some of the 51 million displaced persons in our world.

O'Connell concludes her book with the observation:

> [I]nternational law needs improvement, not demolition, because it remains the single, generally accepted means to solve the world's problems. These problems will not be solved by armed conflict or the imposition of a single ideology or religion. Through international law diverse cultures can reach consensus about the moral norms that we should commonly

> live by. People everywhere believe in law, believe in this alternative to force, as they believe in higher things. They want the power of law to be used to achieve the community's most important common goals. International law reflects that the international community's shared goals are peace, respect for human rights, prosperity, and the protection of the natural environment.[61]

International law, statesmanship, moral leadership by civil society, including the churches can all contribute to a developing consensus about the moral norms that we should commonly live by, securing our national borders while being responsive to our obligations to those less fortunate than ourselves because they find themselves on the wrong side of our borders plagued by persecution. I return to Australia accepting that my political leaders will always maintain a commitment to stopping the boats, no matter what political party they represent; but I return insisting that there is a need for international co-operation to determine how decently to stop the boats while providing an increased commitment to the orderly transfer of an increased number of refugees across our border so that they might live safe and fulfilling lives contributing to the life of the nation.

This cannot be done in Australia until we shut down the processing centres on Nauru and on Manus Island, until we accept that people should only be held in detention while issues of identity, security and health are determined, and while we negotiate arrangements with Indonesia, India and any other transit countries to which asylum seekers are being returned, replicating the new European regulation:

> No person shall, in contravention of the principle of *non-refoulement*, be disembarked in, forced to enter, conducted to or otherwise handed over to the authorities of a country where, inter alia, there is a serious risk that he or she would be subjected to the death penalty, torture, persecution or other inhuman or degrading treatment or punishment, or where his or her life or freedom would be threatened on account of his or her race, religion, nationality, sexual orientation, membership of a particular social group or political opinion, or from which there is a serious risk of an expulsion, removal

---

61. Mary Ellen O'Connell, *The Power and Purpose of International Law* (Oxford: Oxford University Press, 2011, 370.

or extradition to another country in contravention of the principle of *non-refoulement*.⁶²

It might then be possible for Australian officials to conduct prompt, reliable onboard assessments of asylum seekers on vessels determining whether it is appropriate to return them to their last port of call, without the need for an onboard international lawyer to conduct any sort of 'framing' exercise. It should then be possible to avoid the recent obscene scenario of 157 persons being detained on the high seas for a month, regardless of whether or not the non-refoulement obligation applies extra-territorially.

International law has its place in helping to change the policy settings of governments and to redirect the public debate. No doubt the *Hirsi* decision helped contribute to the development of thinking in Europe culminating in this recent regulation for dealing with boat people coming across the Mediterranean. It remains to be seen how effective Frontex Operation Triton is both at dissuading people from setting out on boats in the first place and then rescuing them when they do. With 280,000 people having entered the European Union illegally in 2014, it is no surprise that the European Union is now experimenting with its own externalized border, seeking to have Niger, Tunisia, Egypt, Morocco and Turkey prescreen intending migrants.⁶³ The United Kingdom continues to be agnostic about the utility of proactive interception and rescue missions on the Mediterranean. When Operation Triton was being established, Baroness Anelay, the Minister of State, Foreign and Commonwealth Office, told the House of Lords:

> We do not support planned search and rescue operations in the Mediterranean. We believe that they create an unintended 'pull factor', encouraging more migrants to attempt the dangerous sea crossing and thereby leading to more tragic and unnecessary deaths. The Government believes the most effective way to prevent refugees and migrants attempting this dangerous crossing is to focus our attention on countries of

---

62. Article 4(1), Regulation (EU) No 656/2014 of the European Parliament and of the Council, 15 May 2014.
63. See http://www.thenewstribune.com/2015/04/01/3719274/african-envoy-expresses-concern.html#storylink=cpy

origin and transit, as well as taking steps to fight the people smugglers who wilfully put lives at risk by packing migrants into unseaworthy boats.[64]

The Spanish Parliament has now legislated to allow 'hot returns' of irregular migrants at the Spanish enclaves of Ceuta and Melilla in North Africa 'in order to prevent illegal immigration into Spain'. The borders of these enclaves are guarded by the Spanish border police and Moroccan forces. Stefan Kessler, the Europe senior policy officer for the Jesuit Refugee Service, says, 'There is the concrete danger that persons will be physically prevented from reaching the border crossing points and therefore will be blocked from lodging a protection claim'.

When considering the mission of international lawyers trying to humanise these externalised borders, I call to mind Martii Koskenniemi's prescient remarks:

> International law increasingly appears as that which resists being reduced to a technique of governance. When international lawyers are interviewed on the Iraqi war, or on torture, or on trade and environment, on poverty and disease in Africa—as they increasingly are—they are not expected to engage in hair-splitting technical analyses. Instead, they are called upon to soothe anxious souls, to give voice to frustration and outrage. Moral pathos and religion frequently fail as vocabularies of engagement, providers of 'empty signifiers' for expressing commitment and solidarity. Foreign policy may connote party rule. This is why international law may often appear as the only available surface over which managerial governance may be challenged, the sole vocabulary with a horizon of transcendence—even if, or perhaps precisely because, that horizon is not easily translated into another institutional project. I often think of international law as a kind of secular faith.[65]

None of us would want more realistic and more decent options in these most toxic of times to be forfeited simply because there is a new

---

64. House of Lords, *Hansard*, 15 October 2014, Column WA41.
65. Martti Koskenniemi, 'The Fate of Public International Law: Between Technique and Politics' (2007) 70(1) *Modern Law Review* 1 at 30.

emerging fundamentalism being preached by the most respected high priests of international law. It is time to concede that none of us has a right to enter another country and that all of us have the obligation not to return anyone presenting at our border to a situation of persecution, torture, or cruel punishment. Though I doubt the possibility of the European Union negotiating appropriate returns of asylum seekers to Libya in the foreseeable future, I continue to entertain the hope that Australia can negotiate appropriate returns to transit countries such as Indonesia for Iraqis, Afghans and Iranians and India for Tamils, so that Australia might then decently extend the hand of welcome to more of the world's 51 million displaced persons. For the moment, my country is failing to strike the right balance between human rights and the national interest. It is stopping the boats indecently, violating the human dignity of those being held in unsatisfactory conditions in Papua New Guinea and on Nauru and failing to ensure appropriate safeguards are in place for the return of asylum seekers to Indonesia. For as long as international lawyers claim there is no possibility of a legally negotiated regional agreement for safe returns because they argue that asylum seekers have a right of entry to Australia to seek asylum, the Australian government, the Australian parliament, and the Australian courts will maintain, with impunity but with the occasional expression of outrage from international lawyers, a regime of returns insufficiently scrutinised for human rights compliance. I return to Australia accepting that the boats will continue to be stopped (no matter which political party is in power), but that they should be stopped decently and in compliance with the legal regime enunciated by the European Union which has to deal with a far more pressing issue but subject to the more searching supervision of the European Court of Human Rights and of the European Parliament which has greater sensitivity to the human rights of asylum seekers than do their more pragmatic Australian colleagues.

By all means, stop the boats. But also close the facilities on Nauru and in Papua New Guinea. Abandon the Cambodian shipment plan. Negotiate a regional agreement for safe returns ensuring compliance with the non-refoulement obligation. Double the refugee and humanitarian component from 13,750 places to 27,000 places in the migration program, as recommended by the 2012 Expert Panel.

Encourage further community participation in a refugee resettlement scheme which allows refugee communities and their supporters to increase the number of refugees resettled without taking the places of those refugees who would come anyway without community sponsorship. Why not increase the humanitarian program to at least the 20,000 places which were guaranteed prior to the election of the Abbott Government? And provide another 7,000 places for community sponsored refugees. I agree with novelist Tim Winton that there is a need for countries like Australia to turn back, to 'raise us back up to our best selves'. That can best be done by securing our borders and increasing our commitment to orderly resettlement of more refugees, rather than by opening the borders, undermining the community's commitment to further assisting more of those 51 million people who are suffering displacement, most of them having no prospect of employing a people smuggler to get them to the border of a rich democratic country.

A Comment on
Human Rights and the National Interest:

The case study of asylum, migration and national border protection

Mary Ellen O'Connell

It is a privilege to comment on this case study of asylum, migration and national border protection. Fr Brennan is a true expert on the law most relevant to the study—international refugee law. Refugee law is a highly complex area of international law and not one in which I am expert. Nevertheless, I have been called upon in the past to think about the challenges of implementing, enforcing and amending refugee law from the perspective of an international law generalist. That is the approach I take again here, hoping it is of some value in thinking about the important questions of concern to Fr Brennan. My focus here will be narrower than his, seeking only to comment on what international law requires when desperate human beings seek to reach places of safety and prosperity where they are not citizens.

This comment makes four points with respect to Fr Brennan's approach and international law: First, his conclusion that 'stopping the boats is a precondition to finding a politically acceptable, compassionate and fair solution' is consistent with the fundamental legal and moral principle at stake: the human right to life. Second, stopping the boats means stopping them before they leave shore. Once they do, all ships, including those of the Australian Navy, have a duty based on rules separate from refugee law to save lives. On board an official vessel, the flag state has jurisdiction over the rescued person and is required to apply relevant refugee law and international human rights law. Third, Fr Brennan is right, in my view, that some in the legal community, while well intentioned, seem nevertheless to exaggerate the extent of state obligations under refugee law and IHRL. Finally, while I agree with his analysis and proposals for the short term, I want to add that it is also essential to address the deeper causes of today's migration crisis. Armed conflict and climate change are both linked to why people flee. Responding to these challenges, especially by renewing knowledge and respect for general international law, is an integral part of any effective effort respecting migration, refugees, and national borders.

Stop the Boats

Fr Brennan begins with a confession of error. He believes that he was wrong to support certain changes to Australia's refugee law in view of the fact that between 2005 and 2013 some 1,200 people lost their lives at sea while attempting to reach Australian shores. His humility is an example for all. In this book he sets out his new position, which focuses centrally on saving the lives of people who might drown at sea. He makes a powerful case for stopping the boats as a matter of urgent priority. I agree and take the same view respecting other places in the world where people are attempting to traverse open seas in small boats or cross vast territory by other risky means of transportation. The *Guardian* has reported that in the first quarter of 2015, 500 migrants drowned in the Mediterranean alone. That number is ten times higher than in the same period in the previous year.[1] Saving lives immediately needs to be the priority, and that means preventing small, inadequate boats from setting out into the sea, as well as preventing children from climbing on to moving trains, and the like. On this, Fr Brennan and I agree. We also agree that prevention can and should be enforced consistently with international law.

Save Lives at Sea

Our position on prevention may put us at odds with some in the international human rights and refugee law community. Any disagreement, however, should not be seen as terribly extensive. Fr Brennan is correct that the obligations of the *Refugee Convention* do not apply extra-territorially. Rescue ships, even official ones, are not the territory of a state. Nevertheless, other international rules require

---

1. *Record Number of Migrants Expected to Drown in Mediterranean this Year*, Guardian, April 1, 2015, available at http://www.theguardian.com/world/2015/apr/01/record-number-of-migrants-expected-to-drown-in-mediterranean-this-year.

the extension of *Refugee Convention* and human rights protections to rescued persons on board official ships.

Preventing boats from leaving shore will at times fail and unseaworthy vessels will get into trouble or be abandoned by venal captains and crews at sea. At that point, all masters of ships have an international legal responsibility to attempt to rescue all whose lives are in peril. According to the 1982 United Nations Convention on the Law of the Sea (UNCLOS), Article 98(1):

> Every State shall require the master of a ship flying its flag, in so far as he can do so without serious danger to the ship, the crew or the passengers:
>
> (a) to render assistance to any person found at sea in danger of being lost;
>
> (b) to proceed with all possible speed to the rescue of persons in distress, if informed of their need of assistance, in so far as such action may reasonably be expected of him.

Most provisions of UNCLOS, including this one, are considered binding even on states, like the United States, not party to the Convention as rules of customary international law.[2]

Once an individual is on board an official vessel of any sort, such as navy, coast guard, or fishery enforcement, the state whose flag the ship flies acquires jurisdiction to a certain extent over the individual. With jurisdiction comes the obligation to extend relevant human rights and *Refugee Convention* protections owed by the state to that individual. Recent cases in the European Court of Human Rights explain that states must respect human rights of even non-nationals beyond a state's borders if the state exercises control over the person or the space where the person is present.[3] The state has both of these forms of control with respect to persons on board official ships.

The most important obligation of international refugee law, and this is arguably also a rule of customary international law, is

---

2. See also the 1974 International Convention for the Safety of Life at Sea (SOLAS Convention) and the International Maritime Organization, et al, *Rescue at Sea, A Guide to Principles and Practices as Applied to Refugees and Migrants* (Jan 2015).
3. See *Al-Skeini v. United Kingdom,* App No 55721/07, 53 Eur HR Rep 589 (2011).

not to return individuals to places where they will be persecuted. International human rights law protects persons from being returned to places where they may suffer torture, as well as cruel, inhuman and degrading treatment. In order to ensure returnees will not subjected to torture or other cruel treatment, the official ship's state must do at least a basic review of the rescued person's situation and have knowledge of places where rescued persons might potentially be landed by the ship.

The conditions in the place of landing must be known because of states' duties under human rights law. The flag state may well have no obligation to admit the person to its own territory. Still, it may not disembark the person where she might suffer serious human rights abuse, such as becoming a victim of torture.[4]

In the decision that Fr Brennan discusses, *Sale v. Haitian Refugee Centers Council, Inc*, the United States Supreme Court held that Haitians rescued in the Caribbean by United States Navy ships could be forcibly returned to Haiti with no review of any kind. The decision is simply wrong. Scholars may be reluctant to point this out so directly, owing to the concern that if states must carry out on-board reviews, they might avoid rescuing migrants. As mentioned at the outset of this section, however, all ships must rescue. Moreover, allowing policy ends to influence how we interpret or discuss the law is part of the underlying problem, in my view, respecting international law today. The law is regularly interpreted with an eye to various desiderata and not what it actually says on the basis of standard interpretation principles and authority. This is a growing problem that undermines respect for international law and the sense of the legitimacy and binding nature of international legal obligations—a subject that will be discussed further in the final section of this comment.

Finally, we also hear that regardless of the legal obligation, carrying out this dual review is too burdensome. This objection, too, should be rejected. Review is the law. While it is true that reviewing the situations of hundreds or even thousands of people onboard official vessels will require resources, countries like the United States or Australia clearly have plenty of resources for activities to which

---

4. See James C Hathaway and Michelle Foster, *The Law of Refugee Status*, 25-39 (second edition 2015).

they give priority. A single Reaper drone costs about $14 million USD in 2015.

Advocating Authentic International Law

Much of Fr Brennan's discussion concerns his worry about inaccurate interpretations of human rights law and refugee law that are, in reality, advocacy for more rights for migrants. I have observed a similar approach by lawyers and law scholars trying to expand the category of *jus cogens* norms beyond what the evidence will bear in an attempt to create stronger rights for individuals.[5] Of even greater concern to me is the attempt to reinterpret the United Nations Charter prohibition on the use of force. In recent years, even human rights advocates have argued the Charter should be found to allow the use of military force for humanitarian intervention. National security lawyers also advocate exceptions and re-interpretation of the prohibition on force to fight terrorism, for arms control, to punish, or to wreak revenge.

Unlike Fr Brennan, I do not see a 'new fundamentalism' in international law. Rather, I see a growing tendency to manipulate and misrepresent international law in the interest of various agendas, something that is the opposite of strict application of the law. This tendency will lead to international law becoming of little use. When the law is open to subjective claims, it loses the objectivity and stability that critically distinguish law from policy or politics. My response is to revive international legal education. Knowing what the law actually requires and the reasons to value law in the international community will do more to support human rights, the environment, and peace than unsupported claims about state obligations or rights.

Respond to the Causes

The previous comment about reviving knowledge and respect for international law is related to another important point with respect to saving lives. Despite the advocates, international law still prohibits the resort to military force against other states and intervention on

---

5. See, Mary Ellen O'Connell, *Jus Cogens, International Law's Higher Ethical Norms, in* The Role of Ethics in International Law 78 (Donald Earl Childress III ed Cambridge, 2011).

the side of rebels in civil war. Yet, wars are continuing and escalating. War is currently generating the largest numbers of migrants who flee to safety, often on small boats. Migrants also flee the economic consequences of climate change—droughts, floods, disease, wars over water rights, fishing rights, grazing rights, and oil. People in the United States and Australia who feel no responsibility for migrants seeking refuge apparently fail to see the connection between the unlawful invasion of Iraq in 2003, the disproportionate use of force in Afghanistan since 2001, the greenhouse gasses poured into the atmosphere in violation of the 1992 United Nations Framework Convention on Climate Change, and other serious violations of international law.

If these leading states had led on international law, how many desperate people would have remained safely at home?

Conclusion
Fr Frank's short-term prescriptions are sound. It is imperative that they be based on the most accurate, most dispassionate view of the law. There is a duty to rescue; there is a duty to extend human rights and refugee law protections to persons under a state's jurisdiction. Strict compliance with international law will redound to the benefit of states. International law forbids the use of military force; it requires protection of the environment. Respect for this law provides the world's best chance for a future in which humanity and the natural world will flourish everywhere.

Conclusion

Having an Assured Place Informing Public Policy and Law Making

The public holiday for Martin Luther King's birthday on 19 January 2015 was a much more political affair than it has been in recent years. The spate of police killings of young African American men such as occurred at Ferguson caused the whole country to take pause, wondering what is happening in race relations. Then came the 50th anniversary of the first of the voting right marches across the Edmund Pettus bridge in Selma, Alabama. Ultimately King led those marchers to Montgomery, the state capital, seeking the franchise for all Americans. The movie *Selma* was launched over the long weekend of the King birthday holiday. It's a great study in race relations even though it is marred by a too simplistic condemnation of President Lyndon B Johnson who was doing all he could to secure the changes through Congress. The change required action both by King and Johnson. It is often that way.

On the Boston College campus, faculty and students gathered to talk about race in modern America. They held a wonderful celebration of song, dance and stirring evangelical rhetoric led by the Reverend Brandon Crowley, pastor of the Myrtle Baptist Church. That stirring black Baptist preaching was a change from the usual Jesuit preaching on the campus! The celebration was called 'Wade in the Water', the title of one of the old negro spiritual hymns which draws on the Old Testament Exodus theme of crossing the sea to freedom, as well as the scene in John's gospel at the pool of the Sheep Gate: 'From time to time an angel of the Lord would come down and stir up the waters. The first one into the pool after each such disturbance would be cured of whatever disease they had.'

I had the opportunity to visit the grand monument to King in Washington DC earlier in my stay, when the weather was kinder. I also stood at the spot in front of the Lincoln Memorial where King delivered his 'I have a dream' speech in August 1963. Each time I have called King to mind, I have remembered his letter to the white clergy he sent from Birmingham Jail earlier in 1963. I have been challenged and inspired by his observations about the role and stance of the 'white moderate'. He wrote to his white fellow clergy:

> I must confess that over the last few years I have been gravely disappointed with the white moderate. I have almost reached the regrettable conclusion that the Negro's great stumbling block in the stride toward freedom is not the White Citizens Councillor or the Ku Klux Klanner but the white moderate who is more devoted to order than to justice; who prefers a negative peace which is the absence of tension to a positive peace which is the presence of justice; who constantly says, 'I agree with you in the goal you seek, but I can't agree with your methods of direct action'; who paternalistically feels that he can set the timetable for another man's freedom; who lives by the myth of time; and who constantly advises the Negro to wait until a 'more convenient season.' Shallow understanding from people of good will is more frustrating than absolute misunderstanding from people of ill will. Lukewarm acceptance is much more bewildering than outright rejection.[1]

Being a white moderate, his challenge has stayed with me. The African American Congressman John Lewis who led the first of the bloody Selma marches had the honour of standing on the bridge and introducing the black president Barak Obama who walked the bridge with his wife Michelle, daughters Malia and Sasha, in company with his predecessor George W Bush and wife Laura. Obama spoke with great religious and nationalist fervour. Recalling the bloody events of fifty years ago, he said, 'It was not a clash of armies, but a clash of wills'. Lewis and his fellow marchers 'kept marching towards justice'. The marchers singing their gospel songs were Christian and Jew, black and white, young and old. Obama acknowledged the presence in the

---

1. Martin Luther King Jr, 'Letter From a Birmingham Jail', 16 April 1963 at < http://okra.stanford.edu/transcription/document_images/undecided/630416-019.pdf>.

crowd of the white journalist Bill Plante who had covered the march fifty years ago writing the observation, 'The growing number of white people lowered the quality of the singing'. Obama surmised, 'To those who marched though, those gospel songs must never have sounded so sweet' and eventually 'their chorus would reach President Johnson'. Change did come but 'many in power condemned rather than praised them'. They were called everything 'but the names their parents gave them. Their faith was questioned. Their lives were threatened. Their patriotism was challenged.'

To those who think there is no longer a race problem in the US, Obama said, 'Ferguson is not just an isolated incident.' To those who think there has been no change, he said that incidents like Ferguson are 'no longer endemic, or sanctioned by law and custom'. Obama put the challenge, 'We know the march is not yet over' and he provided the hope: 'laws can be passed, and consciences can be stirred, and consensus can be built'.

Good race relations still has a long way to go in the USA; so too in Australia. The police thin blue line is often a good place to start when reflecting on the issue. Aboriginal imprisonment rates in Australia are still a national disgrace. They are worse than when the Royal Commission into Aboriginal Deaths in Custody was convened. We Australians also need to wade in the water. We need the co-operation of the Johnsons and the Kings. All parties need to be at the table, listening respectfully before committing to joint action.

Fr Gasson spent his last six years of life living and working in Montreal, Canada. He spent some of that time teaching at Loyola High School, a Jesuit school in Montreal. He would have been very surprised by recent developments at Loyola which has become one of the nodal points for carving out the space for people to thrive on difference in the midst of the secular liberal agenda for individual autonomy and non-discrimination. Loyola is one of the few unashamedly Catholic secondary schools remaining in Quebec. The school's website header carries a quote from the school principal: 'A Loyola education is not intended to prepare students for the world but to prepare students who will change the world'. While I was the holder of the Gasson Chair at Boston College in 2014-2015, Loyola High had an important, but partial, win in the Supreme Court of Canada upholding freedom of religion.

The increasingly secularist Quebec government has designed a curriculum for all schools dealing with ethics and religious culture (ERC). The ERC's objectives are the 'recognition of others' and the 'pursuit of the common good'. The ERC includes materials on all world religions, and on all systems of ethical thinking (religious and non-religious). The ERC stresses that all people possess equal value and dignity and it seeks to foster the shared values of human rights and democracy. By rolling out the ERC, the Quebec government hopes that all students will develop an openness to diversity and respect for others. Private schools are able to apply for an exemption from the fixed ERC curriculum if they can satisfy the minister that their alternative course meets the objectives of the ERC.

On 18 March 2008, Loyola High School applied for exemption from the ERC explaining to the minister:

> The program that you have proposed for implementation has as one of its goals the promotion of tolerance and respect for all. The program we offer our students promotes this value in a way that is fully in keeping with the Catholic mission of the school. We have promoted the knowledge and respect of other beliefs in the teaching of World Religions, and have done so for many years. In short, our students are strongly formed in the key values that the new program proposes but this formation is accomplished in a way that is in keeping with the Catholic Faith and moral values that are at the core of the school. This is what our parents expect and desire for their sons.
>
> Given our unique status as the only remaining Catholic school for English speaking boys, and, according to theological and legal opinion, it seems to us entirely appropriate and a proper expression of Religious Freedom to be exempted from this program.

This application triggered a seven year court battle all the way up to the Supreme Court of Canada. Loyola asserted the right to teach Catholic doctrine and ethics from a Catholic perspective. Loyola informed the Supreme Court that it 'did not object to teaching *other* world religions objectively in the first component which focuses on 'understanding religious culture.' As their counsel pointed out to the court, 'You can't teach Buddhism from the Catholic point of view' and 'there is no issue with the way the program requires world religions to be taught'. But Loyola 'wanted to be able to teach the *ethics* of other religious traditions from the perspective of the Catholic religion rather than in an objective and neutral way.'

All seven judges sitting on the Supreme Court case decided that it would be a totally unwarranted interference with the freedom of religion to require the teachers at Loyola High School to teach Catholicism in an objective or neutral way. This would amount to 'requiring a Catholic institution to speak about Catholicism in terms defined by the state rather than by its own understanding of Catholicism'.

Justice Abela writing for four of the judges said:

> Part of secularism is respect for religious differences. A secular state does not—and cannot—interfere with the beliefs or practices of a religious group unless they conflict with or harm overriding public interests . . . The pursuit of secular values means respecting the right to hold and manifest different religious beliefs. A secular state respects religious differences, it does not seek to extinguish them.[2]

However these four judges in the majority thought that there was a limit to the freedom of a Catholic school teaching its own 'take' on other ethical systems. These judges decided that there would be 'no significant impairment of freedom of religion in requiring Loyola to offer a course that explains the beliefs, ethics and practices of other religions in as objective and neutral a way as possible, rather than from the Catholic perspective.'[3] They could see no problem with 'requiring Loyola to teach about the ethics of *other* religions in a neutral, historical and phenomenological way'.

The four judge majority of the court decided that the Quebec Minister's decision to deny Loyola an exemption from the ERC was unreasonable and that the Minister would now need to reconsider the school's application ensuring only that there was freedom to teach Catholicism as the school pleased.

---

2. *Loyola High School v. Quebec (Attorney General)*, 2015 SCC 12, [43].
3. *Loyola High School v. Quebec (Attorney General)*, 2015 SCC 12, [6].

The other three judges would have gone further in Loyola's favor, granting the school's application for complete exemption from the ERC immediately. These judges were clearly very impressed with the school's commitment to respectful and informed discussion of other world religions. The school was able to demonstrate to the court that religious leaders of other faiths were regular and honoured guests at the school. In considering whether teachers at a Catholic school could be required to teach schoolboys the ethics of another religion in a neutral way, Chief Justice McLachlin writing for these three judges observed:

> For Catholic teachers at a Catholic school, the forced neutral posture poses an unenviable choice: they can express a neutral (and therefore insincere) viewpoint on an ethical question that touches on a precept of the Catholic faith, or they can simply remain silent. Neither insincerity nor silence is conducive to the ERC Program's objectives of promoting individual deliberation and the exchange of ideas.[4]

The Chief Justice said that 'requiring a religious school to present the viewpoints of other religions as equally legitimate and equally credible is incompatible with religious freedom'[5]. Admittedly it is only in Canada that one would expect such questions of pedagogy to be agitated all the way to the Supreme Court. On hearing of the decision, an Australian Jesuit wrote to me saying: 'Amazing when you have to go to Court to see common sense prevail'; and an American Jesuit wrote saying: 'I was amazed that the issue could ever arise. If only our invasion of Canada in 1812 had been successful, our Canadian cousins would have been spared having to wrestle with the matter.' Seven years on, it is heartening that the Jesuits, their teachers and parents can get on with the task of preparing students who will change the world—even in Quebec. Hopefully there will always be a place for cultivating what Pope John Paul II called 'a convinced and pondered trust in the heritage of virtues and values handed down' by the forebears of the students presenting at a Catholic school.

---

4. *Loyola High School v. Quebec (Attorney General)*, 2015 SCC 12, [159].
5. *Loyola High School v. Quebec (Attorney General)*, 2015 SCC 12, [160].

When I first studied at Georgetown University Law School twenty years ago, one of my mentors was Fr Ladislas Orsy SJ. While holding the Gasson Chair at Boston College in 2014–2015, I had the opportunity to meet again with Las. Now in his 90s, he gave me a copy of his last published article entitled 'The Divine Dignity of Human Persons in *Dignitatis Humanae*'.[6] It is Las's reaffirmation that Vatican II is the Church's affirmation of belief in the human person who has a conscience. Orsy is a great advocate for true human freedom as the precondition for human flousihing and the thriving of any society buttressed by the rule of law. He espouses individual freedom:

> Persons are free internally when their spirit in its deliberations, decisions, and actions is independent, when it is not imposed or hampered by an outside agent or by their own unruly passions. They are free externally when no outside power coerces them physically or sets up obstacles for their intended actions.[7]

While being a great advocate of human freedom and individual virtue, Orsy makes no claims to human infallibility. He observes, 'Integrity does not guarantee the truth of a judgment or the prudence of an intended action. For that it must rely on critical intelligence. The task of conscience is not to create infallible knowledge or unfailing wisdom but to keep a person faithful to his or her honestly acquired conviction.'[8] Having had a year away from the Australian public square, I had the time and space to appropriate what Las would call the grace of integrity, knowing that I was returning to a church scene and a public square which is often very sterile, bereft, and unanchored. All any of us religious believers can bring to the public square is our integrity and inner freedom, together with our simple faith that God is with us giving us hope as we go forward. After a lifetime of engagement in the Church and the public square, Orsy writes:

---

6. Ladislas Orsy, 'The Divine Dignity of Human Persons in *Dignitatis Humanae*', in *Theological Studies* 2014, 75/1 (2014): 8–22.
7. Orsy, 17.
8. Orsy, 16.

> Persons have integrity when their inner being is transfused by harmony; when their decisions and actions flow from their honest judgment; when they faithfully pursue the values that they comprehend as means to their perfection. In contrast, they lose their integrity when their volitions and operations are divorced from their vision. Should such a disaster happen, the persons in question become traitors to themselves. Their inner world shatters; it becomes fragmented.
>
> Integrity, however, does not mean that the individual judgments held by persons of integrity are by that fact alone correct and critically unassailable. Quite the opposite: their convictions must be open to critical examination and verification.[9]

I return to Australia open to dialogue with anybody, happy to have my convictions questioned and verified, and free on my part to question especially those who exercise authority. Without freedom and integrity, there is nothing any of us can contribute to the swirling mess of institutions which have lost public confidence, including the hierarchical church and the materialistic secularist public square which is marred by short term political conniving, an increasingly isolated and sterile jurisprudence, and a titillating shallow media. We are called into trusting, honest, self-disclosing dialogue with those seeking human flourishing for all, regardless of the utterances and strategies of those who enjoy short term power and success. We need to proclaim in comprehensible language and with incarnated symbolism the breaking in of the kingdom of God here and now. And we need to do this, grounded in our social reality, alert to the claims of those who are marginalised and suffering ongoing injustice.

---

9. Orsy, 15.

Contributors

James F Keenan, SJ is the Canisius Chair, Director of the Jesuit Institute and Director of the Gabelli Presidential Scholars Program at Boston College. A Jesuit priest since 1982, he received a licentiate and a doctorate from the Pontifical Gregorian University in Rome. He has edited or written 18 books and published over 300 essays, articles, and reviews in over twenty-five international journals. He has been a Fellow at the Institute of Advanced Studies at The University of Edinburgh, the Center of Theological Inquiry, Princeton, and the Instituto Trentino di Cultura. Fr Keenan is the founder of Catholic Theological Ethics in the World Church (CTEWC) and chaired the First International Cross-cultural Conference for Catholic Theological Ethicists in Padua, Italy. Following that experience, he hosted another international conference of theological ethicists in Trento, Italy. Today CTEWC is a live network of over 1000 Catholic ethicists (www.catholicethics.com). His most recent book is *University Ethics: How Colleges Can Build and Benefit from a Culture of Ethics* (Rowman and Littlefield, 2015). He is presently writing another book, *A Brief History of Catholic Ethics* (Paulist Press).

Mary Ellen O'Connell is the Robert and Marion Short Professor of Law and is Research Professor of International Dispute Resolution-Kroc Institute for International Peace Studies at the University of Notre Dame. Her research is in the areas of international legal theory, international law on the use of force, and international dispute resolution. She is the author or editor of numerous books and articles on these subjects, including, *What is War? An Investigation in the Wake of 9/11* (Martinus Nijhof/Brill, 2012) and *The Power and Purpose of International Law, Insights from the Theory and Practice of*

Enforcement (Oxford 2008, paperback 2011). She is currently at work on a book project, *The Art of Law and Peace*. She has degrees from Northwestern; LSE, Cambridge (where she was a Marshall Scholar) and Columbia, where she was Louis Henkin's teaching and research assistant.

Margaret Somerville is Samuel Gale Professor of Law, Professor in the Faculty of Medicine, and Founding Director of the Centre for Medicine, Ethics and Law at McGill University, Montreal, where she has taught since 1978. Her books include: *The Ethical Canary: Science, Society and the Human Spirit* (Penguin 2000); *Death Talk: The Case Against Euthanasia and Physician-Assisted Suicide* (MQUP 2002); and *The Ethical Imagination: Journeys of the Human Spirit* (Anansi 2006), which she delivered as the nationally broadcast CBC 2006 Massey Lectures. Her forthcoming book is *Bird on an Ethics Wire: Battles about Values in the Culture Wars* (MQUP 2015). She consults, nationally and internationally, to a wide variety of bodies. She is a Fellow of the Royal Society of Canada. In 2003 she was the first recipient of the UNESCO Avicenna Prize for Ethics in Science and in 2013 was awarded the Queen Elizabeth II Diamond Jubilee Medal for services to higher education.

Index

A

Abbott Government, 71, 109.
Abbott, Tony, 97, 98.
Abela, Justice, 39, 121.
abortion, 4, 14, 15.
agnosticism, 7.
Alito, Justice, 14
Alzheimer's disease, 35,
amicus brief, 4, 14, 15, 86.
Anelay, Baroness, 106.
Aristotle, Paris, 76.
Assisted Dying Bill, 47, 48, 49, 52.
assisted reproductive technologies (ART's), 58, 59.
asylum, xiii, xv, 8, 9, 13, 69–116.
atheism, 7, 22.
autonomous choice, 35.

B

Barth, Robert, x.
Benedict XVI, Pope, 18, 19.
Biggar, Nigel, 32, 33, 51, 52.
Bingham, Lord, 89, 90, 91.
Border protection, 9, 10, 69–114.
Boston College, ix, x, xi, xiii, xiv, 13, 23, 70, 117, 119, 123, 125.
Bush, George W, 80, 81, 118.

C

Callahan, Daniel, 54.
Cameron, Clyde, 102.
Carens, Joseph, 72, 73, 74.
Carter case, 42, 44, 45, 57, 58, 61, 63, 66.
Carter, Kay, 40, 50.
Cass, Moss, 102.
Catechism of the Catholic Church, 16, 93.
Charter of Rights and Freedoms, Canadian, 39, 40.
child sexual abuse, 19.
Christmas Island, 8, 96.
civil society, 18, 32, 105.
Clinton, Bill, 80, 81.
Committee Against Torture, 87.
common good, xi, xii, 1, 3, 12, 15, 19, 20, 27, 32, 33, 36, 51, 55, 57, 58, 61, 63, 64, 65, 66, 120,

compassion, xii, 7, 16, 19, 34, 35, 55, 60, 98, 103, 104, 111.
comprehensive world view, 1.
conscience, 8, 14, 18, 19, 22, 23, 25, 119, 123.
Convention against Torture, 78.
CPCF v Minister for Immigration and Border Protection, 91, 92, 93.
Criminal Code, Canadian, 57.
criminal law, 35, 40, 41, 46, 61, 78.
culture, xii, 2, 3, 18, 19, 20, 21, 25, 38, 44, 76, 100, 104, 120.
Cuomo, Mario, 17, 18.

D

Declaration of Montreal, 66.
dementia, 35, 45, 48.
Deus Caritas Est, 18, 19.
Dignitatis Humanae, 6, 123.
dignity, xi, xii, 6, 9, 12, 13, 16, 22, 25, 33, 35, 39, 49, 55, 59, 66, 75, 99, 108, 120, 123.
Dignity and Choice in Dying, 49.
disability, 13, 35, 36, 45, 50, 61, 62.
discrimination, xv, 1, 3, 5, 16, 34, 36, 55, 58, 61, 65, 66, 119.
DNA, 28, 29, 60.
Dulles, Avery, x.

E

Ellacuria, Ignacio, 23,
embryos, 27, 29, 30, 31, 32, 59.
Ethics and religious culture (ERC), 120-122

European Convention on Human Rights, 46, 94, 95, 96,
European Court of Human Rights, 79, 92, 95, 96, 113.
euthanasia, 47, 59, 61, 62.
Evangelium Vitae, 18.
exceptionalism, 89.

F

Falconer, Lord, 47, 48, 49, 52.
Faircloth, Sean, 22.
Finnis, John, 7.
Forché Carolyn, 23.
Francisco, Jose Mario, x.
Francis, Pope, xv, 8, 10, 11, 16, 17, 18, 19, 20, 21, 22, 24, 100.
Fraser, Malcolm, 101, 102, 103, 104.

G

Gasson, Thomas, ix, x, xiii,
genetic manipulation, 31, 58, 59.
Gillard Government, 71.
globalization, 86, 100.
Goodwin-Gill, Guy, 78, 80–89, 91.
Grayling, AC, 22.
Greenawalt, Kent, 13.
Gummow, Justice, 79, 89, 90.

H

Habermas, Jürgen, 1, 2, 60.
Harris, John, 32.
Heaney, Seamus, 99.
High Court, Australian, 79, 86, 87, 89–93, 97,

Hirsi v Italy, 93.
Hollenbach, David, v, 4, 55.
Hope of Craighead, Lord, 90.
Howard Government, 70.
Human Fertilisation and Embryology Act, 29.
human germ line, 31, 57, 59.
Human Rights Act, 93, 96.
human rights, xiv, 1, 2, 7, 55, 58, 65, 78, 81, 84, 87, 92, 98, 11–116.
human rights law, 105, 112.
Humanae vitae, 10, 11, 12, 24.
hypocrisy, 18, 100.

I

International Covenant on Civil and Political Rights, 78, 79.
international law, 75, 76, 78, 79, 80, 82, 83, 85, 87, 88, 89, 93, 97, 98, 104, 105, 106, 108, 111, 113, 115, 116.
international co-operation, 102, 105,
IVF, 29, 31, 32.

J

Jesuit Refugee Service, 107.
Joffe, Lord, 47, 48.
John Paul II, Pope, xv, 18, 122.
justice, xiv, 4, 6, 7, 9, 18, 19, 20, 21, 23, 24, 33, 39, 40, 41, 50, 62, 77, 118, 124.

K

Kant, Immanuel, 12
Kennedy, Justice, 16, 17.
Kessler, Stefan, 107.
King, Martin Luther, 117, 118.
KINO Border Initiative, Nogales, 69.
Koskenniemi, Martii, 107.
Kurt, Joseph, 15.

L

Lamb, Paul, 49, 50, 55.
Lampedusa, xv, 8, 93, 100.
Laudato Si', 19, 20, 24.
liberty, 1, 2, 4, 14, 40, 41, 60, 62.
Lou Gehrig's Disease, 37, 39, 46.
Loyola College, xiii,
Looyola High School, 119, 120-122.

M

MacKellar, Michael, 102, 103.
Mahoney, Jack, 30, 32.
Manus Island, 8, 105.
Maternal spindle transfer, 27, 30.
McLachlin, Justice, 122
McNelis, Paul, x.
McPhee, Ian, 103.
Mendez, Juan, 97, 98.
Monan, Donald, 23, 24.
moral leadership, 105.

N

Nauru, 8, 74, 87, 105, 108.
national sovereignty, 72,
Neuberger, Lord, 48, 95.

Nicklinson, Tom, 47, 48, 49, 50, 51, 55.
Nicolas, Aldolfo, 20, 21.
Nitschke, Philip, 48.
non-refoulement, 73, 89, 90, 105, 106, 108.
Nurse, Robert, 28.

O

O'Connell, Mary Ellen, 75, 76, 104, 105, 111–116, 125.
O'Malley, John, x, 25
O'Malley, Martin, 13, 14.
O'Malley, Sean Patrick, 8, 69.
O'Neill, Baroness, 52.
Obama, Barack, 118, 119.
Obergefell v Hodges, 14, 15, 16, 17.
Orsy, Ladislas, 123.

P

Pannick, Lord, 49.
Papua New Guinea, 74, 76, 108.
parenthood, 11, 12.
Paul VII, Pope, 10, 11, 24.
Pellegrino, Ed, 34.
physician assisted suicide (E/PAS), xiii, 3, 6, 27, 34, 41, 43, 45, 46, 47, 50, 51, 53, 54, 57, 58, 61, 62, 63, 65.
pluralism, 21.
pluralist society, xiv, 6.
political justification, 2.
political philosophy, 1.
political political theory, 9, 10, 33.
political virtue, 9, 10, 33.
precept, 13, 34, 122.

pro-nuclear transfer (PNT), 27, 29, 30.
public affairs, 10, 17, 29, 34.
public morality, xiii, 6, 12, 13, 17.
public square, xiv, 1, 2, 7, 8, 13, 18, 19, 32, 98, 123, 124.
purification of reason, 18, 19.

R

Rawls, John, 1, 2, 7.
realism, xii, 103, 104.
refoulement, 83, 90, 105.
refugee, 73, 78, 83, 85, 89, 90, 91, 92, 112, 113.
Refugee Convention, 78, 79, 82, 83, 85, 86, 88, 89, 90, 91, 92, 95, 96, 112, 113.
Refugee law, 85, 112, 116.
Rehnquist, Chief Justice, 36, 37, 38, 43, 46.
Rodriguez case, 63.
Rodriguez, Sue, 37, 38, 55.
Roe v Wade, 15.
Romero, Oscar, 23.
Royal Commission into Aboriginal Deaths in Custody, 119.
Rudd, Kevin, 70, 71, 76, 77.

S

sacred and secular, 14.
Sale v Haitian Centers Council, 81, 91, 114.
same sex marriage, xiv, 3, 5, 6, 14, 15, 16, 17.
same sex parents, 5.
self-determining decision, 35.

Shannon, Jim, 28.
Sherrington, John, 29, 31.
Sopinka, Justice, 37.
Souter, Justice, 45.
statesmanship, 105.
suicide, 35–55, 62, 63, 64, 65.
Sulston, John, 28.
Sumption, Lord, 51
Supreme Court, Canadian, 37, 38, 40, 42, 43, 44, 45, 46, 47, 50, 54, 57, 61, 63, 64, 66, 119, 120, 121.
Supreme Court, United Kingdom, 48, 49, 51,
Supreme Court, United States, 4, 5, 6, 14, 37, 45, 50, 65, 80, 81, 82, 85, 86, 87, 92, 93, 114.
Supreme Court, Victoria, 95.
Swift, Jonathan, 53.

T

Tampering with Asylum, 70, 71.
Taylor, Gloria, 39, 40, 42, 50, 55.
terminally ill, 36, 37, 38, 46, 47, 49, 54.
turn back the boats, 77, 87.

U

UNCLOS, 113.
UNHCR, 70, 74, 82, 83, 85, 86, 88, 89, 90, 91, 102.
United Nations Human Rights Council, 91, 97, 98.
USCCB, 15, 16.

V

Vacco v Quill, 43, 44.
Vatican II, 24, 25, 123.
Verbessem, Eddy and Marc, 44.
Veritatis Splendor, 18.
Vietnam War, 70, 101.

W

Waldron, Jeremy, 2, 3, 9, 10, 33.
Warnock, Baroness, 28, 32.
Washington v Glucksberg, 36, 37, 45, 46, 50.
Whitlam, Gough, 101, 102.

Lightning Source UK Ltd.
Milton Keynes UK
UKOW01f0442070218
317473UK00002B/199/P